# Corporate Interiors

No. 6

**Above:** Game Show Network, Santa Monica, CA.
**Design firm:** Hellmuth, Obata + Kassabaum, P.C.

# Corporate Interiors

No. 6

Roger Yee

Visual Reference Publications Inc., New York

Visual Reference Publications Inc.
302 Fifth Avenue
New York, NY 10001

Distributors to the trade in the United States and Canada
Watson-Guptill
770 Broadway
New York, NY 10003

Distributors outside the United States and Canada
HarperCollins International
10 East 53rd Street
New York, NY 10022-5299

Library of Congress Cataloging in Publication Data:
Corporate Interiors No. 6

Printed in China

The book is exclusively distributed in China
by Beijing Designerbooks Co., Ltd.
Building No.2, No.3, Babukou, Gulouxidajie,
Xicheng District, Beijing 100009, P.R.China
Tel: 0086(010)6406-7653   Fax: 0086(010)6406-0931
E-mail: info@designerbooks.net
http://www.designerbooks.net

ISBN: 1-58471-075-6

Book Design: Priscilla Sue Mascia

# CONTENTS

# Introduction

# No *"right"* way to design today's office?

Hey, America. You invented the skyscraper in the late 19th century. How's the view down there?

Of the six tallest buildings that will be towering above the world between now and 2009, just two are in the United States. Chicago's Sears Tower is the shortest at 1,450 feet. In ascending order, the other current and future title holders will be the Petronas Towers (1,483 feet), in Kuala Lumpur, Malaysia; Shanghai World Finance Center (1,614 feet), under construction in Shanghai, China; Taipei 101 (1,670 feet), the world's tallest building in 2005, in Taipei, Taiwan; the Freedom Tower (1,776 feet), under construction in New York; and Burj Dubai (over 2,000 feet, with its final height a secret), under construction in Dubai, United Arab Emirates. What dramatizes this race to the sky is the proliferation of architectural languages to describe extreme height. Gone is the simple rectangular shaft. The new skyscrapers curve, twist, slant, step back and display numerous other spatial inventions as they climb.

## There is no "right" way to design a skyscraper today.

Similarly, there's no "right" way to design an office as the 21st century begins. True, the traditional office environment, split between private offices, fiefdoms defined by full-height walls and doors for managers and professionals, and bullpens, undivided seas of desks for secretaries and clerks, has lost favor. Taking its place is the open-plan office, blending a handful of private offices for managers with a multitude of open-plan work stations for everyone else, using partial-height partitions without doors to separate individual desks or work stations. But look closely, and the choices are less obvious. Some private offices, for example, double as conference rooms. There are also open-plan work stations that are little more than touchdown spots. Casual meeting areas and coffee bars increasingly break up the rigidity of office grids. No longer does "one size fits all." A lot of experimenting is going on.

What this means is that organizations need architects and interior designers more than ever to create offices that support their specific ways of working. Why should today's workforce, staffed by rising percentages of college graduates, women, minorities and working parents, struggle with dysfunctional, rigid and pre-computer era workplaces? That's why five editions ago *Corporate Interiors* was launched , introducing business executives to America's leading architects and interior designers serving major corporations and institutions worldwide.

Inevitably, some offices portrayed in this latest edition, Corporate Interiors No. 6, remain firmly traditional by choice, while others appear aggressively avant garde. What enables you to work best? Take a tour of the outstanding new corporate and institutional facilities that appear on the following pages. You may find more than a few talented design firms whose work and ideas could inspire your next office.

Roger Yee
Editor

# AREA

550 South Hope Street
Floor 18
Los Angeles, CA 90071
213.623.8909
213.623.4275 (Fax)
www.areaarchitecture.com

# AREA

Herman Miller Los Angeles Design Center
Los Angeles, California

**Above left:** A/V meeting room.
**Above right:** Pantry/lounge.
**Opposite:** Cross bracing detail.
**Photography:** Jon
Miller/Hedrich Blessing

When you're Herman Miller, America's second largest office furniture manufacturer, working with AREA to renovate and expand a 10,000-square foot showroom at the Los Angeles Design Center on a tight budget in time for NeoCon West, a major trade show, it is business as usual. Key steps in the recently finished project, demolishing the wall isolating the existing kitchen to create an open, interactive pantry/lounge, and upgrading the audio-visual meeting room with a screen and other A/V equipment that would function as design elements, have given the space its fresh, dynamic appearance—particularly when demolition revealed cross bracing that now enlivens the pantry/lounge. The meeting room, similarly inspired by the cross bracing, is sheathed in glass at skewed angles and features a dramatic glass A/V screen serving as "environmental sculpture" beneath an undulating suspended ceiling. Who says speed plus economy can't equal good design?

# AREA

## Clifford Chance US LLP
## San Francisco, California

**Top left:** Reception desk.

**Above left:** Lounge.

**Above right:** Reception and main conference room.

**Opposite below right:** Open and private offices.

**Photography:** Jon Miller/Hedrich Blessing

A handsome example of the growing foreign presence in American business districts is the new, 54,000-square foot, three-floor San Francisco office for 140 employees of Clifford Chance, designed by AREA. Clifford Chance, a global law firm based in the United Kingdom with a 7,300-person staff, including 602 law partners, wanted its West Coast headquarters to project a regional image that would simultaneously reflect its historic European culture and its adherence to a progressive yet casual business atmosphere.

The successful solution combines a modern interpretation of classic simplicity, lightness of color, and geometric subtlety with extensive use of glass in the reception area and conference center, giving employees and visitors sweeping views of Treasure Island and the Oakland Bridge, careful selection of building materials and methods to assure environmental safety and renewability of resources, and sparing use of precious materials. In any culture, it says welcome.

**AREA**  Reed Smith LLP
Los Angeles, California

One hundred, twenty-five-plus years is a respectable age for a top international law firm that prides itself on a dedication to core values of teamwork, professionalism and mutual respect. However, having served many clients for years with a high level of personal service doesn't require the firm of Reed Smith to look venerable as well. Which is why AREA was commissioned to design its new, 46,500-square foot, two-story, 120-person Los Angeles office as a progressive environment that nods respectfully towards its history but looks unmistakably to the present and future in providing attorneys' offices, open plan work stations, reception area, conference center, library and support spaces. The sophisticated new image created for Reed Smith is the sum of numerous thoughtful details. Its neutral, white overall setting, for example enriched with wood accents; glass block walls and adjacent vision panels admit light to interior conference rooms while avoiding the "goldfish bowl" effect;

# AREA

**Right:** Open work stations.

**Below:** Corridor.

An existing stair structure employs fritted glass panels to add a veiled atmosphere to the reception area; and ambient lighting in all public spaces heightens awareness of the facility's vertical space and reduces glare. For a firm founded in Pittsburgh in 1877 that now employs nearly 100 lawyers in the United States and Great Britain, the Los Angeles office is ready for whatever the second century demands.

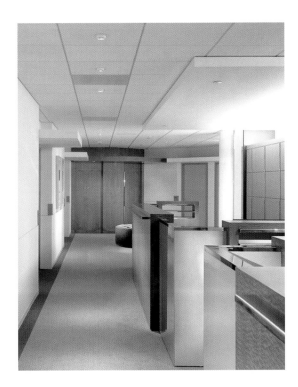

# Aref & Associates Design Studio

100 N. Sepulveda Blvd.
Suite 100
El Segundo, CA 90245
310.414.1000
310.414.1099 (Fax)
www.aref.com

## Aref & Associates Design Studio  Christensen, Miller, Fink, Jacobs, Glaser, Weil & Shapiro, LLP
Los Angeles, California

Whether corporate chieftains and entertainment industry moguls will find themselves facing one another in the conference rooms at the Los Angeles law firm of Christensen, Miller, Fink, Jacobs, Glaser, Weil & Shapiro is purely conjectural. However, the firm's new, 65,000-square foot, three-story office in the MGM Tower for some 220 people, designed by Aref & Associates, acknowledges the intriguing possibility. The contemporary, functional and flexible facilities include private attorneys' offices, secretarial workstations, conference rooms, war rooms and computer room, highlighted by a videoconfer-

ence center where CEOs can feel at home, amidst breakout rooms planned for mergers-and-acquisitions transactions, mediation and arbitration. Simultaneously, such materials as the movingue wood trim, neutral walls accented with vibrant artwork, sparkling stone flooring, etched and clear glass, and carpet create an open, airy, cutting-edge image that reflects the dynamics of entertainment law. Since Christensen, Miller has a strong entertainment practice, the quality of its new workplace has created the kind of positive buzz in the entertainment industry that the attorneys like to hear.

**Aref & Associates Design Studio**     Gibson, Dunn & Crutcher LLP
Los Angeles, California

Consistently ranked among the world's top law firms by its peers, Los Angeles-based Gibson, Dunn & Crutcher represents clients that include some of the world's largest multinational corporations, leading government entities and major commercial and investment banks. For the Westside neighborhood of Los Angeles, the firm's new, 27,000-square foot Century City Offices for 80 employees, designed by Aref & Associates, projects an open, spacious and welcoming modern image. The private attorneys' offices, teaming secretarial workstations, and conference center with breakout room and full video conferencing capability, appointed in such materials as fiddleback makore wood trim, stone flooring, and etched, clear and cast glass, give Gibson, Dunn a functional, flexible and ergonomic workplace to serve power brokers in America's second most populous city.

**Above Left:** Conference room.
**Above:** Main reception area.
**Right:** General offices.
**Left:** Point workstation
**Photography:** Paul Bielenberg.

# Aref & Associates Design Studio

G4 Media, Inc.
Los Angeles, California

Video game enthusiasts think they're in paradise at the new, 78,000-square foot, two-level, 220-person offices of G4 Media in Los Angeles, designed by Aref & Associates. G4 Media owns and operates G4techTV, a cable television network airing news and entertainment programs on video games that parent company Comcast launched when it purchased and merged TechTV (formerly ZDTV) with its subsidiary G4 high-technology channel. A production studio and creative workspace form the heart of G4's new facility, which includes private offices, collaborative teaming workstations, game capture, conference rooms, and computer room. To nurture G4's very young work force, the design team has created a whimsical, open and airy workplace that encourages collaborative teaming, informal communication and productive effort. As a result, the space reflects the lively spirit of video games, using wood, stained concrete, clear glass, carpet tile, neutral and intense colors and images of video game icons to furnish an interior that is the envy of the video game community.

**Opposite upper left:**
Boardroom.

**Opposite lower left:** Reception
with video game kiosks.

**Opposite far left:** Commons.

**Photography:** Paul Bielenberg.

## Aref & Associates Design Studio

Kilroy Realty Corporation
El Segundo, California

Kilroy Realty Corporation has owned, operated, developed, and acquired Class A suburban office and industrial real estate, primarily in southern California, since 1947. So the company knows when and why office buildings age—and how to restore them to Class A status. A good example is the turnaround of Kilroy's 909 and 999 Buildings in El Segundo, two aging structures that were recently upgraded by Aref & Associates.

Entrances and lobbies have been given a fresh, new image through contemporary renovations featuring marble, granite, wood veneer, fabric upholstered walls, custom furnishings and sophisticated lighting. In addition, the west side of the 909 Building now looks at an existing parking structure that has been enhanced by a creative, billboard art wall evoking El Segundo's aerospace industry, and new signature red numbers give

both buildings greater stature. How has the market responded? Leasing has increased as dramatically as the properties' visibility.

**Above:** Entrance lobby.
**Right:** Exterior of 999.
**Photography:** Paul Bielenberg.

# A/R Environetics Group, Inc.

116 East 27th Street
New York, NY 10016
212.679.8100
212.685.9044 (Fax)
www.arenvironetics.com

A/R Environetics Group, Inc.

# A/R Environetics Group, Inc.

## Magnet Communications
## New York, New York

**Top left:** Reception/Boardroom.

**Top right:** Enclosed workstations.

**Above:** Open area.

**Right:** Pantry/Breakout rooms.

**Opposite:** Conference pod.

**Photography:** Norman McGrath.

Rated by PRWeek as one of America's top 22 public relations agencies, Magnet Communications serves such diverse clients as the Anaheim Angels, Bombay Sapphire, Elizabeth Arden Red Door Salons & Spas, IBM, KFC, Oxford Health Plans and Pioneer New Media Technologies. To maintain the creative edge of its New York head-quarters, Magnet recently invited A/R Environetics Group to design an open, flexible, 45,000-square foot office in six renovated factory buildings for 220 employees, retaining the rawness of the existing loft space. Not only did Magnet eliminate most private offices, it placed private client and in-house meetings in enclosures that would contrast with the existing brick arches and vaults, concrete columns and vaults, structural timber and exposed ceilings. Low-profile work stations clustered around columns, "enclosed workstations" in sheetrock, metal and glass without ceilings along the perimeter, and sleek, 15-foot diameter, circular "conference pods" of metal and glass, whose air-conditioned interiors of white-board and fabric-paneled walls, carpeted floors and pendant lighting evoke space stations, sustain lively communications that are open in more ways than one.

# A/R Environetics Group, Inc.

## Swiss Re Financial Services Corp.
## New York, New York

**Left:** Trading Area.

**Below left:** Video conference room.

**Below right:** Reception.

**Opposite:** Corridor with illuminated glass floor and glass corner.

**Photography:** David Joseph.

There's little room for error in trading rooms—the stressful, high-stakes environments where well trained and aggressive traders buy and sell millions of dollars' worth of securities every business day with the help of sophisticated computers, telephones and information services, plus robust mechanical and electrical systems. So when Swiss Re Financial Services Corporation and A/R Environetics Group developed a new, 31,000-square foot New York office encompassing a trading floor and support space for 220 employees, the facility clearly had to make its triangular-shaped building work

at maximum efficiency. Taking prudent risks has generously rewarded the Financial Services Business Group of Swiss Re, one of the world's leading reinsurers, and the new, single-floor facility is exemplary. Key points of the beech wood, stainless steel and glass interior include the circulation corridor that wraps around the building's triangular core to separate public and private areas while unifying the entire space, raised floor for heavy data cabling, large soffits above trading desks that integrate the mechanical systems, and service spaces that feed off the circulation corridor so trad-

ing desks, private offices and conference rooms can have perimeter windows that put Swiss Re and its personnel in a very good light.

# A/R Environetics Group, Inc.

Ferragamo USA
New York, New York

**Upper left:** Workstations with custom display niche.

**Upper right:** Reception desk with display case.

**Left:** Open plan workstation.

**Opposite:** Executive office.

**Below right:** Building Lobby.

**Photography:** David Joseph, Mario Carrieri.

In a precisely choreographed operation resembling a fashion industry runway show, Ferragamo USA, the New York-based subsidiary of Salvatore Ferragamo Inc., the Italian fashion house of elegant footwear, handbags, designer clothing and accessories, recently completed the remodeling of its 22,500-square foot, eight-story Manhattan building and 12,000-square foot New Jersey facility without interrupting its 150-person operations. The company's design firm, A/R Environetics Group, established a multi-phased, two-and-a-half-year project to keep employees moving ahead of construction crews. Consequently, the New York building's lobby and reception area, private offices, open plan work stations, conference rooms and pantries form an ideal backdrop for Ferragamo's products, incorporating a touch of the company's signature red as an accent for such appointments as walnut wood, Italian limestone, stainless steel, glass and display cases where product samples can stage daily shows of their own.

# A/R Environetics Group, Inc.

## Milestone Merchant Partners
New York, New York

Refined International Style-design, good planning, and a dramatic view from Manhattan's legendary Seagram Building have produced a splendid, 7,000-square foot New York office for the employees of Milestone Merchant Partners, a full-service merchant bank headquartered in Washington, D.C. that provides investment banking, restructuring and related advisory services to middle market businesses. The key to the new environment, designed by A/R Environetics Group, has been a fresh, cost-effective interpretation of the building's classic Modernist detailing, created in 1958 by Ludwig Mies van der Rohe with Philip Johnson. An understated setting of deep archways in dark walnut, stainless steel and white glass establishes the drama of the central reception room and boardroom that separate the executive and main office spaces, and a glass wall in the reception area draws visitors to the breathtaking panorama of Park Avenue, the heart of the nation's business center.

**Top:** Reception area.

**Above:** Executive office.

**Right:** Boardroom as seen from reception.

**Photography:** David Joseph.

# BergerRait

411 Fifth Avenue
New York, NY 10016
212.993.9000
212.993.9001 (Fax)
www.bergerrait.com

## BergerRait

Bloomberg, LP
New York, New York

Bloomberg, LP, a worldwide financial communications company with 8,000 employees serving customers in 126 countries, represents a special challenge to the interior design firm that maintains its space. For BergerRait, which has supplied on-call design and management services to Bloomberg since 1999, remodeling and updating this dynamic and growing media leader's workplaces in two Manhattan buildings, 499 Park Avenue and 110 East 59th Street, has required creative and functional design solutions that are informed by constant monitoring and communications and delivered on tight schedules to meet high design standards. In the latest example, BergerRait designed 300,000 square feet of contemporary facilities on 10 floors for 1,200 employees at open-plan work stations. The resulting environment has proved as exciting as it is effective. Here, staff members can work comfortably alone or within groups; non-hierarchical, open-plan areas are anchored by shared conference rooms and central areas for coffee and snack breaks; and newly finished, state-of-the-art broadcast and production facilities emerge from construction without interrupting office activities around them. How many companies can reinforce a global brand identity with a great place to work like this?

**Top right:** Coffee and snack bar.
**Above left:** Interior stair.
**Above right:** Production facility.
**Opposite:** Atrium.
**Photography:** Mark Ross.

**BergerRait**

Martha Stewart Living Omnimedia
New York, New York

**Top left:** Private office.

**Top right:** Conference room.

**Left:** Test kitchen.

**Above:** Commons.

**Opposite:** Open-plan office area.

While the 150,000-square foot, one-story Manhattan office for some 500 employees of Martha Stewart Living Omnimedia doesn't resemble the domestic settings that appear in the media company's books, magazines, catalogues, television programs and product packaging, it has been planned, designed and constructed with the same, meticulous care. BergerRait, serving in the role of associate architect to the firm of Daniel Rowen Architect, has provided space planning, design development, construction documents and project management for this ambitious facility within the Starrett Lehigh Building, an Art Deco-style industrial landmark structure. The award-winning space uses an "open architecture" approach to planning that preserves much of the powerful, original interior architecture while providing maximum flexibility and deep penetration of natural light and views to such facilities as photography studios, test kitchens, prop library, woodworking shop, merchandising center, computer facilities, and open-plan and private offices. The offices themselves are specially configured to maintain the overall feeling of openness. For example, a custom-made work station for open areas has been created from an industrial "kit of parts" to encourage communication and collaboration. As for private offices, they are located along the interior with full-height glass fronts to take advantage of the inward transfer of natural light. Quite impressive for a behind-the-scenes workspace that the company's customers will never see.

**BergerRait**

Schwartz & Benjamin
New York, New York

Women might consider their footwear as works of art—especially if they could tour the New York showroom of Schwartz & Benjamin on West 57th Street. Occupying two consecutive floors that once housed art galleries, the 10,000-square foot sales and design office of the 82-year-old, Massachusetts-based shoe importer, wholesaler and distributor displays the shoes it designs and sells as a licensee to Kate Spade, Anne Klein and Michael Kors against a backdrop of all-white,

minimally-detailed and gallery-like interiors. Indeed, the facility, comprising three showrooms, design studio and archives for vintage shoes, makes good use of its column-free, high-ceiling space by receiving visitors in a memorable way as soon as they arrive at the striking reception area along the 4th

**Above:** Showroom.

**Right:** Reception.

**Opposite:** Stairway detail.

**Photography:** Mark Ross.

# BergerRait

floor window wall and its views of West 57th Street. From a small seating area furnished with examples of classic Modern furniture beside a sculptural steel stairway rising out of a rock garden, they can ascend to the corporate and design offices on the 5th floor. Full-height, sliding, lacquered panels acting as room dividers give showrooms privacy or remain open to emphasize the gallery-like quality of the space. Since every showroom detail counts, the design is finished in elegantly tailored, gray and white-toned surfaces of concrete, stone, lacquer and wood that form an ideal packaging for the shoes on display.

**Above left:** Vintage shoe archives.

**Above right:** View of reception from stairway.

**Top right:** Sales work station.

# CBT/Childs Bertman Tseckares Inc.

110 Canal Street
Boston, MA 02114
617.262.4354
617.236.0378 (Fax)
www.cbtarchitects.com

CBT/Childs Bertman Tseckares Inc.

# CBT/Childs Bertman Tseckares, Inc.

## Wolf, Greenfield & Sacks, P.C.
## Boston, Massachusetts

Intellectual property has been Wolf, Greenfield & Sacks, P.C. sole focus for over 75 years, and its innovative approach to practice is visible in its new, 60,500- square-foot, four-story office created by CBT/Childs Bertman Tseckares, Inc. Wolf Greenfield's office projects a sense of creativity, modernity, and flexibility achieved through ample use of glass, open spaces, curving corridors, exotic materials like zebrawood for panels, and a surprising punctuation of space with points of bold color. CBT's design not only projects a clean, modern image of the company, but the use of translucent resin materials, customized with inset flowers, and the many glass-encased conference rooms, allow for privacy without obstructing the abundant natural light.

**Above left:** Conference rooms.
**Above right:** Entrance lobby.
**Right:** Staircase.
**Below right:** Reception desk.
**Opposite:** Reception and conference room.
**Photography:** Anton Grassl.

# CBT/Childs Bertman Tseckares Inc.

Abrams Capital
Boston, Massachusetts

CBT/Childs Bertman Tseckares, Inc. designed the office of Abrams Capital, a capital management firm in Boston, to reflect an intimate and comfortable space accoutered in stone, leather, glass, and rich, dark wenge wood. These materials and other traditional elements introduced through the colors, materials, and outlines of the furniture soften a modern and transparent aesthetic that met the firms need for visual access throughout. The office includes conference space and private offices, living room, trading area, fitness facility, along with a reception and a seating area offering spectacular views of the Charles River and Boston's historic Back Bay neighborhood.

**Top:** Reception.
**Above:** Views from living room.
**Left:** Main conference room.
**Opposite:** Seating.
**Photography:** Anton Grassl.

## CBT/Childs Bertman Tseckares, Inc.

First Marblehead
Boston, Massachusetts

**Right:** Conference rooms and seating area.

**Bottom Right:** Workspaces.

**Bottom:** Detail.

**Photography:** Edward Jacoby.

Founded in 1991 and headquartered in Boston, First Marblehead sought a space design that better serves its evolving business and operational requirements and embodies their public image. To promote open communication and team-work among employees, CBT/Childs Bertman Tseckares' design of the 30,000-square foot workspace bears similarities to a trading floor. Central to the firm's identity is the transparency of its operations. With this in mind CBT designed a spacious and airy workplace of open workstations, reception areas and cafe, meanwhile enclosing meeting rooms, conference rooms and individual offices in glass to preserve openness while providing privacy. Rich colors and dark tiger wood-paneling help to maintain a professional environment, while custom furniture and unique fixtures convey a modern approach that has made First Marblehead a leader in its field.

## CBT/Childs Bertman Tseckares Inc.

### Brown Rudnick Berlack Israels
Boston, Massachusetts

In the design of Brown Rudnick Berlack Israels' Boston office, CBT/Childs Bertman Tseckares, Inc. was responsible for helping the client to redefine their corporate identity and express their creative approach to business. The forward-looking, bold image they wanted to project through their office centers on a dramatic black-and-white mural design by artist Sol LeWitt. The program for the 125,000-square-feet of space involved the redesign of three floors, to include a new multi-media event center with advanced audio-visual and teleconferencing capabilities and custom-designed furniture integrating the technology, restacked support space, and additional office space. The contemporary theme of the reception lobby repeats throughout the firm and is reflected in the details of the winding stair leading to upper-level conference and seating areas. The use of clear glass maximizes natural light, suggesting an openness throughout the firm.

**Top left:** Conference room and seating area.

**Upper left:** Multi-media center.

**Above left:** Lounge.

**Above right:** Lobby.

**Photography:** Anton Grassl.

47

# CBT/Childs Bertman Tseckares Inc.

Goulston & Storrs
Boston, Massachusetts

**Above:** Reception.
**Right:** Elevator lobby.
**Below:** Private office.
**Photography:** Anton Grassl.

Goulston & Storrs, selected CBT/Childs Bertman Tseckares, Inc. to unify the long, large floor of their new 60,000-square-feet office to articulate an aesthetic that was representative of the century-old law firm. The result is a sleek elevator lobby with upholstered walls, which leads into a reception area that is at once comfortable and dramatic, incorporating a warm palette of neutral colors, rich textures, and deep-toned wood to welcome clients while providing a spectacular view of the Boston Harbor. The design anchors the long space by introducing strong architectural elements in the curved shape of the reception desk, echoed at the opposite end of the plan, visually framing and bringing the space together.

# DMJM Rottet

515 South Flower Street
Los Angeles, CA 90071
213.593.8300
213.593.8610 (Fax)
www.dmjmrottet.com

808 Travis Street
Suite 100
Houston, TX 77002
713.221.1830
713.221.1858 (Fax)

405 Howard Street
4th Floor
San Francisco, CA   94105
415-986-1373
415.986-4886 (Fax)

# DMJM Rottet

Paul, Hastings, Janofsky & Walker
New York, New York

An irregularly-structured floorplate in a Manhattan office building, burdened with an off-center core, angled corners and irregular column spacings, has been transformed into a bold, new corporate identity for Paul Hastings, Janofsky & Walker. Paul Hastings, a leading, national law firm with some 950 attorneys serving corporate clients in 15 offices worldwide, retained DMJM Rottet to create a 150,000-square foot, 11-floor office for over 300 attorneys that would consolidate two major New York locations. To effectively house the firm's private and open offices, conference center, law library, filing spaces, pantries and archival facility in a unifying, contemporary environment of "endless space," the design team has concentrated support spaces in the center, located private offices along the perimeter, inserted an interconnecting staircase linking the conference center with attorney floors above, exaggerated distances with forced-perspective corridors, dropped soffits and tapered walls, and installed glass doors, walls, and counter surfaces to reflect and emit light. The results have been so successful, the Los Angeles, San Francisco and Washington, D.C. offices reflect New York's unmistakable glow.

**Above left:** Conference Center.

**Above right:** Staircase detail.

**Top right:** Private office.

**Opposite:** Main reception and conference center.

**Photography:** Michael Moran.

**DMJM Rottet**

Vanco Energy Company
Houston, Texas

Exploring for oil in extremely deep-water conditions requires topographical site mapping and sectional imaging of the earth's strata, and while the resulting exploration charts routinely aid oil and gas exploration and production companies such as Houston's Vanco Energy Company, they have found an exciting use as the inspiration for Vanco's new, 20,500-square foot, one-level world headquarters for 45 employees, designed by DMJM Rottet. The facility's straightforward scheme locates private offices along the perimeter and open office areas in the interior. Less conventional, however, is the architectonic structure and form of the space. By inventing a visual language of layered space based on exploration charts, the design team has created a space full of restless energy, where wall and ceiling surfaces in white-painted drywall slide past one another like tectonic plates, "carving out" glimpses of wood, stone, lighting and carpet much like "fissures" in the earth. Vanco, currently exploring deepwater assets in West Africa, now has a headquarters worth exploring as well.

**Above left:** Front desk in main reception.

**Above right:** Conference room.

**Left:** View from main reception.

**Far left:** Corridor.

**Opposite:** Main reception.

**Photography:** George Lambros

# DMJM Rottet

QAD, Inc.
Carpenteria, California

**Above:** Reception desk.

**Right:** View of corridor showing coffee/copy area.

**Opposite:** Conference center with custom-designed buffet table.

**Photography:** Seth Boyd

Building the equivalent of a better mousetrap for industrial users of enterprise applications software, Pam Lopker, founder and president of QAD, has created a community of satisfied customers with over 5,200 licensed sites worldwide as well as a successful company employing some 1,200 people in 25 countries. Good treatment of employees has been a hallmark of QAD since its founding in 1979, and the new, 125,000-square foot, two-story headquarters, designed by DMJM Rottet and architect Andrew Newmann, on a hillside overlooking the Pacific Ocean in Carpenteria, California strongly reiterates the company's philosophy. Thus, the facility incorporates a fitness center, recreation room, outdoor recreational facilities and cafeteria, along with private and open offices, conference rooms, and a 35,000-square foot Dealer Briefing Center, featuring an 80-person, multi-tiered auditorium. As the design clearly shows, paying attention to people and technology is a winning combination for QAD.

**Right:** Prefunction area.
**Far right:** Seating area.
**Photography:** Seth Boyd

## DMJM Rottet

### Bernhardt Furniture Company
### New York, New York

**Above:** Living room

**Right:** Entry and reception desk.

**Bottom:** Detail of mirror installation.

**Left:** Core of the showroom.

**Photography:** Paul Warchol

If Tiffany's blue box tied with a white ribbon provides the perfect foil for exquisite jewelry, dinnerware or accessories, the signature white and maple veneer flagship showrooms that Bernhardt Furniture Company operates in Chicago, Los Angeles and New York play a similar role for fine contract furniture made by the family-owned and operated business based in North Carolina. The recently relocated, 10,000-square foot New York showroom, designed by DMJM Rottet, brings Bernhardt to an exclusive space overlooking historic Bryant Park, giving customers spectacular views of Fashion Week and the many other festivities held in this vibrant Beaux Arts garden adjoining the New York Public Library. Yet the showroom is appropriately subtle as a "room with a view," creating a wide range of attractive environments to showcase Bernhardt furniture. Such details as the "Living Room", which accommodates new lounge seating and social gatherings, mirrors that reflect light and expand space, floating shelves that display guest chairs, reveals that define floating planes, and sophisticated lighting give customers ample reasons to direct their gaze indoors.

# Ellerbe Becket, Inc.

800 LaSalle Avenue
Minneapolis, MN 55402
612.376.2000
612.376.2271 (Fax)
www.ellerbebecket.com

**Ellerbe Becket, Inc.**

Target Corporation
Minneapolis, Minnesota

Chic and street-savvy shoppers would expect no less of America's second largest discount retailer. Indeed, Target Plaza South, the new, 1,142,400-square-foot, 32-floor component of Target Corporation's 1,800,000-square foot corporate headquarters in Minneapolis, designed by Ellerbe Becket for some 5,000 employees, epitomizes its motto, "expect more, pay less." The new facility celebrates the workplace as a way to promote communication, a sense of community, and Target's brand identity. At the same time, it provides an efficient, functional and flexible environment that transcends its tight schedule and budget. What surprises visitors is the warmth and intimacy felt in such contrasting spaces as the reception area, open and private offices, conference center, cafeteria, credit union, executive boardroom and suites, and especially, Target Hall. The latter, a casual "family room" featuring a two-story fireplace, large-scale trees, lounge seating, area rugs and skylights, serves as an informal employee gathering

place. Yet Target Plaza South is also a modern office, where versatile furniture systems, configured to reduce the variety and number of work station standards, enable people rather than furniture to move. A central spline simplifies electrical and data distribution, sophisticated lighting and sound masking enhance open offices, formal and informal meeting spaces jointly support teamwork, and security is extensive but unobstrusive. Declares Richard Varda, AIA, ASLA, Target's vice president, store planning and design, architecture and engineering, "The Ellerbe Becket team designed an environment that perfectly reflects Target's corporate culture."

**Above:** Target Hall.

**Opposite above:** Cafeteria, Target Hall fireplace and boardroom.

**Opposite below:** Reception area.

**Photography:** Brian Droege.

# Ellerbe Becket, Inc.

## Gray Plant Mooty
## Minneapolis, Minnesota

Being the oldest continuing law practice in Minneapolis, dating from 1866—as well as one of the most influential—doesn't prevent you from embracing a contemporary vision of the law office. For 500 employees of Gray Plant Mooty who recently occupied a new, 105,000-square-foot, three-level office, designed by Ellerbe Becket, in downtown's landmark IDS Center, new ways of working would include reducing the variety of private and open office sizes, increasing the number of casual meeting and teaming spaces, and sharing the best outside views from floors where few are available. For this reason, the traditional private offices, law library and conference center are supplemented by hoteling offices and war rooms, prime corner locations with views are designed as open teaming spaces, and a lounge and employee break area have been created, complete with kitchen, salt-water fish tank, television and pool table to help employees maintain a healthy work-life balance. Even the conference rooms immediately off the reception area reflect a new sensibility. Among the five conference rooms offering state-of-the-art audio/visual equipment that surround a central pre-function area, one is appointed in comfortable lounge furniture for bereavement and estate planning, a small yet much appreciated new detail.

**Upper left:** Reception.
**Upper right:** Corridor.
**Above:** Break room.
**Opposite:** Elevator lobby.
**Photography:** George Heinrich.

# Ellerbe Becket, Inc.

## PepsiAmericas
## Minneapolis, Minnesota

With the youngest consumers in the United States, Central Europe and the Caribbean knowing the power of brands, there was never any doubt PepsiAmericas, the bottling company that makes, sells and delivers the Pepsi-Cola core brands, Cadbury beverages and other national and regional brands in 18 U.S. locations as well as Puerto Rico, Jamaica, the Bahamas, Trinidad and Tobago, Poland, Hungary, the Czech Republic and the Republic of Slovakia, wanted the Pepsi brand integrated into its newly remodeled, 9,000-square foot, 18-person executive management headquarters in Minneapolis.

The facility's designer, Ellerbe Becket, appreciated this immediately. However, the firm also had to create an appropriate executive environment that would enhance formal and impromptu communications, and support an open corporate culture where executives could excel. The successful manner in which the design team met these goals is visible throughout the facility on the 40th floor of the Dain Rauscher Plaza, from the uncommonly graceful reception area to the handsome open office areas, private offices, conference rooms and break room. While the Pepsi brand appears in the Pepsi logo

on the glass at the entry and the curves in the reception area's ceiling and floor, product display windows are featured in the wood wall between the reception area and the boardroom, glass office fronts brighten corridors, the boardroom boasts advanced audio/visual equipment set within and around a custom table and credenza, and a lively palette of materials has transformed the overall image. For a company that serves over 117 million people, the new design is as refreshing as a Pepsi.

**Above:** Reception area.

**Right:** Wood wall with niches for product displays.

**Opposite above:** Boardroom.

**Opposite below:** Administrative work stations.

**Photography:** George Heinrich

# Ellerbe Becket, Inc.

## Hays Companies
Minneapolis, Minnesota

Fast-growing companies often lack time to expand in an orderly fashion, and insurance broker/risk management consultant Hays Companies, founded in 1994 by James C. Hays and five senior-level individuals from major insurance brokerage firms, typifies this situation. Within two years of its founding, Hays began outgrowing its original 15,000-square-foot space in downtown Minneapolis and started acquiring adjacent office suites on an "as is" basis. Having lived with a proliferation of physical barriers, dysfunctional adjacencies and mismatching aesthetics, Hays retained Ellerbe Becket to design a new, 34,485-square-foot (including a 5,491-square-foot expansion space), single-floor office for 163 employees on an aggressive, seven-month schedule. The new facility, including open and private offices, conference center and employee break area, has won the praises of employees and visitors by providing an efficient and flexible workplace that is also warm and inviting.

# Francis Cauffman Foley Hoffmann, Architects Ltd.

2120 Arch Street
Philadelphia, PA 19103
215.568.8250
215.568.2639 (Fax)
www.fcfh-did.com

Francis Cauffman Foley Hoffmann, Architects Ltd.

# Francis Cauffman Foley Hoffmann, Architects Ltd.

## Dancker, Sellew & Douglas
## Somerville, New Jersey

It's no exaggeration to say that the office environment has changed since Dancker, Sellew & Douglas began serving the New York City region in 1829 as one of its most respected office furniture dealerships. Selling products from Steelcase and its design partnerships, along with such services as furniture rental, warehousing and design consultation, the company asked Francis Cauffman Foley Hoffmann Architects to design its new, 20,000-square-foot, two-story, 85-person home in Somerville, New Jersey as a forward-thinking "integrated interior" and showcase for its expertise, products and services. The new design addresses numerous issues in its general office area, seminar room, break room, presentation room, conference rooms, work/demonstration laboratory, enclaves, touchdown areas and informal team areas. Supported by integrated features such as raised flooring, under-floor HVAC, demountable partitions, plug-and-play communications infrastructure and indirect lighting, DSD can proudly escort customers into a living lab of the 21st century workplace.

**Top left:** Resource library.

**Above left:** View from reception desk to main conference room.

**Above right:** Coffee/informal meeting area.

**Left:** Corridor.

**Opposite:** Reception waiting area.

**Photography:** Don Pearse.

66

# Francis Cauffman Foley Hoffmann, Architects Ltd.

## McNeil Consumer & Specialty Pharmaceuticals
## Fort Washington, PA

As the maker of Tylenol®, McNeil Consumer & Specialty Pharmaceutical knows how the right kind of intervention can change everyday life for the better. This 4,550-square-foot office renovation for a marketing group in Fort Washington, Pennsylvania was the initial project of a company-wide initiative to implement a new, open and dynamic work space that would encourage interaction, collaboration and cross-functional teamwork. The design process was preceded by a strategic workplace study by the architect to understand McNeil's business mission, corporate culture and work processes. As a result, the new facility comprises open work stations, private offices (for directors and above), informal team areas, enclosed team rooms and conference rooms. In a post-occupancy study, 65 percent of respondents believe their new workplace has increased productivity, strongly suggesting that the design is working as prescribed.

**Below:** Informal touch down areas.

**Opposite center:** Open work stations.

**Opposite below:** Informal conference area.

**Photography:** Don Pearse.

## Francis Cauffman Foley Hoffmann, Architects Ltd.

## Telcordia Technologies
Piscataway, New Jersey

A product preview is critical for high technology sales, and the recent renovation of the 12,000-square-foot Customer Briefing Center for Telcordia Technologies in Piscataway, New Jersey, designed by Francis Cauffman Foley Hoffmann Architects, shows it. From the reception area to the offices, presentation rooms and corporate dining room, Telcordia has a sophisticated story to tell organizations that use its flexible, standards-based software and services for IP, wireline, wireless, and cable. But the products that customers preview are not the only focus of the new design. Multiple client groups must also be led along a controlled route and kept apart from each other. Thus, the space provides clear sight lines for presentations, inviting interior furnishings for comfort, a new floor plan that fits the building's column grid, and advanced audio-visual equipment—all prepared under an aggressive budget and schedule. The results so far: Sales are up.

**Top left:** Corridor at prefunction room.

**Above left:** View into demo room.

**Above right:** Entry and reception area.

**Opposite:** Corridor.

**Left:** Dining area.

**Photography:** Don Pearse.

## Francis Cauffman Foley Hoffmann, Architects Ltd.

GlaxoSmithKline
Conshohocken, Pennsylvania

**Right:** Dining area.

**Below:** Conference center breakout area.

**Bottom right :** Executive office.

**Photography:** Don Pearse.

Being on the cutting edge of the pharmaceutical and healthcare industries, multi-billon dollar Glaxo-SmithKline recently exercised its creativity in relocating and consolidating 900 employees in a new, innovative, 200,000-square-foot, five-floor facility at the Renaissance Center in Conshohocken. The project, designed by Francis Cauffman Foley Hoffmann Architects, represents an ambitious exercise in simultaneously reducing space standards to under 200 square feet per person and expanding the percentage of amenity space. Thus, employees circulate among a variety of specially designed environments during the workday, including collaborative team areas, private offices, teaming areas, conference center, video conference suite, cafeteria and company store, with many work areas configured to accept higher densities in the future. As one of the first projects following the merger of Glaxo and SmithKline, the new office presages a healthy future for the expanded enterprise.

# Gary Lee Partners

360 W Superior Street
Chicago, IL 60610
312.640.8300
312.640.8301 (Fax)
www.garyleepartners.com

**Gary Lee Partners**

**Gary Lee Partners**

The Marketing Store
Lombard, Illinois

**Above left:** Reception desk.

**Above right:** Open and private offices.

**Left:** Focus room.

**Opposite:** Reception.

**Photography:** Christopher Barrett/Hedrich Blessing.

If today's brands can truly influence hearts, minds and buying habits, chances are marketing experts such as The Marketing Store are involved. The Marketing Store, an award-winning, international consultant that develops clients' brands through Brand Activation™, recently demonstrated its own agility by teaming with Gary Lee Partners to develop a new, 44,000-square foot, one-story office in Lombard, Illinois for 180 "Brand Activists" who develop toys and marketing promotions for children. Since the company wanted a light, efficient yet professional environment, the private and open offices, focus room and cafeteria establish boundaries without imposing barriers. The design exploits the building's unusual floor plate by establishing quadrants of varying bay sizes to house different departments with work station configurations and color palettes of their own—based on feng shui principles valued by clients in Hong Kong and China. Keeping everything visible with glazed private office fronts, low open office partitions and display areas for "work in progress," the design reminds employees their job is to "make kids smile."

**Gary Lee Partners**

Macquarie Capital Partners LLC
Macquarie Real Estate Inc.
Chicago, Illinois

**Above left:** Conference room.

**Above right:** Reception.

**Left:** View towards private offices.

**Far left:** Open offices.

**Photography:** Scott McDonald/Hedrich Blessing.

Since its founding in 1991, Macquarie Capital Partners has successfully raised capital and won financial advisory assignments for 116 transactions totaling over $21.8 billion. Its new, 18,000-square foot Chicago office, designed by Gary Lee Partners for 30 employees, captures its best qualities, balancing order and openness with privacy. These qualities also succeed in spatial terms, because Macquarie shares its space with Macquarie Real Estate Inc., another division of Macquarie Holdings (USA) Inc., part of Australia's largest investment banking organization, Macquarie Group. Each organization's separate private and open offices, featuring tinted glass divider screens between open work stations and all-glass quiet rooms for privacy, adjoin a shared public area providing reception, conference, mail/copy and lunchroom. To project a contemporary image honoring the financial world's traditions, classic Modern architecture is paired with transitional wood furniture and matching appointments in interiors that cost much less than they appear.

# Gary Lee Partners

A Venture Capital Firm
Chicago, Illinois

How do you create value within a diversified portfolio of companies to achieve attractive returns? For this Venture Capital Firm, a leading private equity investment firm , the successful strategy involves specializing in negotiated investments in profitable, well-managed and growing middle-market companies. Interestingly, the firm's preferred workplace is as traditional as its operations are contemporary, judging from its new, 22,180-square foot office, designed by Gary Lee Partners for some 50 employees on the top floor of a downtown Chicago office tower. The design challenge was to insert a traditional interior, complete with custom mahogany and painted millwork, wood-burning fireplaces in private offices, millwork-clad base building mullions, and furnishings representing various historic periods inside a new, modern building. Yet the functioning of the reception area, private offices, conference center, cigar room and lunchroom makes no compromises with history. Besides being equipped with state-of-

# Gary Lee Partners

the-art technology, the office is flooded with daylight, thanks to such timely features as office fronts with vision glass, administrative stations placed at corners, and wide corridors. If tradition has its place at this firm, so does modernity.

**Above left:** Private office.
**Above right:** Corridor.

# Gensler

| Amsterdam | Detroit | Phoenix |
| --- | --- | --- |
| Arlington | Houston | San Diego |
| Atlanta | La Crosse | San Francisco |
| Baltimore | Las Vegas | San Jose |
| Boston | London | San Ramon |
| Charlotte | Los Angeles | Seattle |
| Chicago | Morristown | Shanghai |
| Dallas | New York | Tokyo |
| Denver | Newport Beach | Washington, DC |

www.gensler.com

**Gensler**

Weil, Gotshal & Manges, LLP
Redwood Shores, California

Technology people in Silicon Valley are so unimpressed by technology that they actually want visual relief from it. Insights like this shape the stunning new, 60,000-square foot, three-floor office for the law firm of Weil, Gotshal & Manges in Redwood Shores, California, designed by Gensler. Staffed by over 1,100 lawyers across the United States, Europe and Asia serving leading companies, Weil, Gotshal takes pride in understanding and working to achieve its clients' key objectives wherever they operate, building on the global strength of three primary departments—Corporate, Litigation/ Re-gulatory and Restructuring—plus an appreciation of local cultures. The new, 60-attorney facility offers a dramatic illustration. Since Weil, Gotshal resides in an area of limited amenities and food services, the design introduces its own destination-style attractions, featuring a popular "living room/community space" with food service, broadcast on a flatscreen monitor and a sense of place. In addition, the high-performance law office is empowered with the latest technology but not dominated by it, focusing on "legal neighborhoods" populated by lawyers, paralegals, secretaries, caserooms, support and high-density filing in close proximity to recreate the collaborative learning environment traditionally provided by the law library. The result is that reception areas, conference center, "living room," private offices, secretarial work stations, and office services (file rooms, copy center, mail room), appointed in backlit and sandblasted glass, wood, stone, and patterned carpet tile, form a contemporary, high-tech, high-touch legal milieu ideal for serving Silicon Valley clients.

**Top right:** Secretarial work station.

**Above left:** "Living room."

**Above right:** Interior stair.

**Opposite:** Reception area and interior stair.

**Photography:** Paul Warchol.

**Gensler**

Absolut Spirits Company
New York, New York

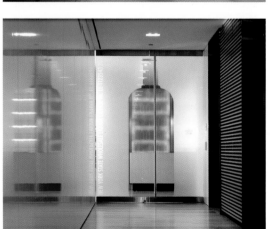

**Top left:** Corridor with commissioned art.

**Above:** Reception area and conference room.

**Above left and left:** Private and open offices.

**Photography:** Nick Merrick/Hedrich Blessing.

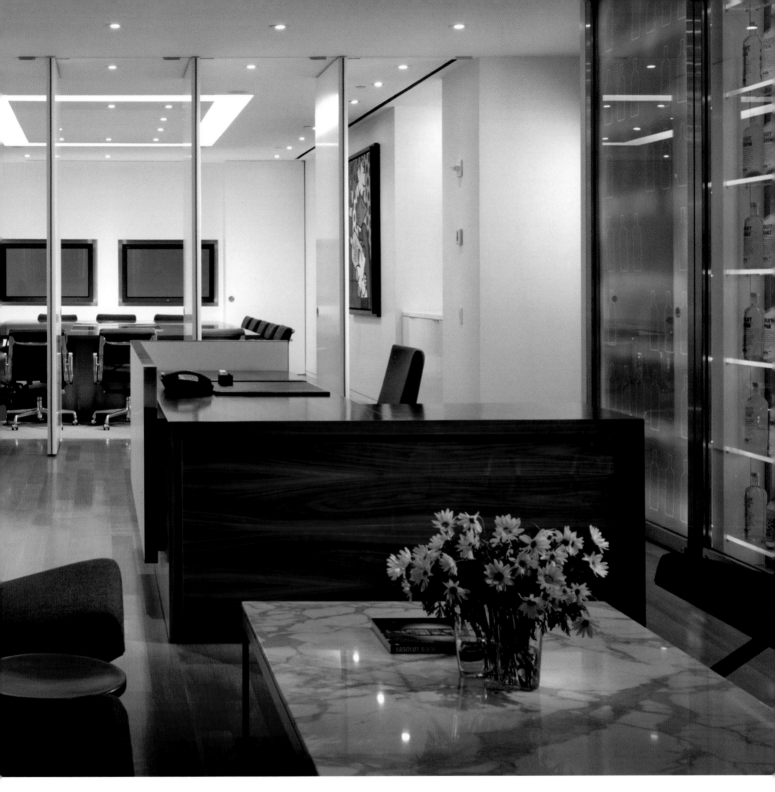

How do you build a U.S. headquarters for an international marketing legend, the Absolut Spirits Company? As designed by Gensler, the new, austerely handsome, 10,000-square foot office for 26 employees embodies the brand's values of clarity, simplicity and perfection, combines respect for the company's Swedish roots and its American workplace, and showcases product and advertising. Of course, the renowned advertising and commissioned art for Absolut—cited among the 20th century's 10 best advertising campaigns by Advertising Age—are conspicuously present, demonstrating their pivotal role in Absolut's success since it was first introduced to the United States in 1979. Yet the clean, simple interior design also testifies to the power of art and design in everyday life. Private offices with clear and translucent glass fronts surrounding an open core and the conference room adjacent to the reception area form an airy and naturally illuminated setting of white lacquered and laminate wall panels and finishes, accented by light oak flooring, oak slat ceilings, Eames and Saarinen seating, Zographos tables--and bracing examples of Absolut advertising, art and bottled spirits.

**Gensler**

Allsteel Inc.
Muscatine, Iowa

**Top left:** One of numerous fireplaces.

**Top right:** Community area.

**Above right:** Boardroom.

**Above left:** Showroom.

**Opposite:** "Silo" multi-purpose creative space.

**Photography:** Chris Barret/ Hedrich-Blessing

In a modern Cinderella story, a former electrical parts plant in a Midwestern community surrounded by farmland has been given a new and vibrant life as a headquarters for Allsteel, a major office furniture maker founded in 1912 that is a division of HNI Corporation. The newly renovated, 65,000-square foot headquarters in Muscatine, Iowa offers more than an opportunity to reestablish Allsteel's independent brand identity as a modern, design-sensitive, Midwestern company. It also supports corporate values of honesty, openness and commitment to customers through four major components, namely an open-plan office area with collaborative pods that reflects a new, non-hierarchical culture, a national training facility for dealers and sales representatives that occupies over a quarter of the building, a showroom for the company's products, and a community center for chance encounters and organized gatherings of employees and community members. Replete with such details as fireplaces from a sister company, architectural shapes reflecting farm community icons and residential furniture in common areas, the award-winning space presents a revitalized Allsteel.

**Gensler**

Baker Botts LLP
Houston, Texas

Change comes soon enough to Baker Botts, the fabled Texas law firm employing some 680 lawyers in practice areas ranging from corporate to litigation to tax law—with a vital niche in energy that reaches such faraway places as Saudi Arabia and Azerbaijan. Consider the new Reception/Conference Center in the Houston headquarters, a 24,500-square foot, single-floor facility designed by Gensler that helps implement a new master plan. To reduce expenses and increase benefits throughout the lease, the new Center consolidates library spaces, reception areas and conference rooms on practice floors and captures space vacated on practice floors for additional lawyers' offices. The new Center reinforces the Baker Botts "brand" by embracing International Style architecture. Yet it is state-of-the-art in every way: wireless and embedded technologies take their place alongside movable walls, multi-use spaces, sophisticated lighting, and such visitors' amenities as multiple data ports, flatscreen TV and private phone booths. Offering meeting rooms of varying sizes and configurations, video-conferencing, caucus areas, visitors' lounge, catering facilities, business center, phone rooms and travelers' storage, the Center has won immediate acceptance by the lawyers, expanded the role of administrative staff and sustained new educational seminars that support the firm's new business model. For a law practice founded in 1840, Baker Botts is well prepared to face the future.

**Above left:** Reception area.

**Right:** Conference rooms and ancillary spaces.

**Photography:** Sherman Takata.

# Gerner Kronick + Valcarcel, Architects, PC

443 Park Avenue South
New York, NY  10016
212.679.6362
212.679.5877 (Fax)
www.gkvarchitects.com

Gerner Kronick + Valcarcel, Architects, PC

# Gerner Kronick + Valcarcel, Architects, PC

## Comedy Central
## New York, New York

**Right:** Main reception.

**Below:** Boardroom.

**Bottom:** Production studio.

**Opposite:** Communicating stair and executive reception.

**Photography:** David Joseph.

Getting serious about fun is the strategy behind the vibrant, new, 75,000-square foot, four-floor (two full floors, two partial floors) New York office of Comedy Central, a cable TV channel owned by Viacom that commands devoted audiences for such programs as "South Park" and "The Daily Show" with Jon Stewart. The interior renovation, designed by Gerner Kronick + Valcarcel Architects, has been complicated by the need to combine offices and production studios on an irregular existing floor plate with interior spaces so deep in the core that they have little exposure to the perimeter. Potential handicaps are overcome by establishing a regular circulation path around the core, opening as many interior spaces to perimeter walls and daylight as possible, and using indirect sources for artificial light. As a result, the facility's reception area, private and open offices, conference rooms, board-room, production studios, coffee bar, pantry and other support spaces, appointed in wood veneer, silver metallic finishes, metal-framed sliding glass doors, and modern, informal furnishings, seem open, accessible and naturally lighted wherever they actually are. Call this good design—and part of the fun at Comedy Central.

**Gerner Kronick + Valcarcel, Architects, PC**    Bear Stearns & Co.
New York, New York

Movers and shakers in global centers of finance know where deals get done. At the new, 1.2-million-square foot, 45-story, 3,000-person New York headquarters of investment bank Bear Stearns & Co., deal makers head straight to floors 12 and 13, where a conference center and executive dining facility set a dignified yet gracious mood. The superbly crafted interiors, designed by Gerner Kronick + Valcarcel Architects within a new office tower from Skidmore, Owings & Merrill, set the stage with architectural millwork, silk wallcoverings, stone and carpeted floors, transitional furnishings and sophisticated lighting, a proper foil for a 1,500-piece art collection. Of course, other, livelier floors for private and open offices, trading floors, cafeteria, auditorium and services are equally handsome and efficient. However, they're not places where deals get done.

**Upper left:** Boardroom.

**Left:** Interiors displaying examples of a 1,500-piece art collection.

**Opposite:** Conference room with prints by Jonathan Borofsky.

**Photography:** Adrian Wilson.

**Below left:** Addition showing air vents.

**Below right:** Clothing/accessories shop.

**Bottom left:** Office area.

**Opposite:** Restored original showroom.

**Photography:** Adrian Wilson.

## Gerner Kronick + Valcarcel, Architects, PC

Mercedes Benz
New York, New York

Savvy New Yorkers know an automobile showroom at 430 Park Avenue that resembles a miniature Solomon R. Guggenheim Museum—boasting a spiraling ramp for three cars—was designed and completed by Frank Lloyd Wright in 1954—two years before he began constructing the Guggenheim. Wright's 3,500-square foot space was originally commissioned by foreign car importer Max Hoffman. Having housed Mercedes Benz for 50 years, the space was recently restored and expanded by the German automaker with

an inspired design by Gerner Kronick + Valcarcel Architects. The makeover offers more than a resurfaced, three-car turntable and a new parapet for the ramp. Two additions, totaling 6,500 square feet, allow Mercedes to display the ultra-luxury ($300,000-plus) Maybach sedan in an elegant, minimal space adjacent to the original showroom, and provide the company a sporty environment in maple, granite, stainless steel and stretch vinyl, separated by the building lobby, for its SUVs, station wagons and sports cars. Has Mercedes ever looked better than this?

**Gerner Kronick + Valcarcel, Architects, PC**  M2L
New York, New York

**Left and above:** Views of the gallery.

**Below left:** Detail of metal and glass wall.

**Photography:** Paul Warchol.

For furniture industry veteran Michael Manes, founder of New York furniture dealership M2L in 1993, modern furniture is as much a passion as a business. Manes represents about 1,200 authorized and licensed furniture pieces created by some 250 architects and designers. To demonstrate the richness of his product line to commercial and residential designers and their clients, he recently added a new, 7,500-square foot, contemporary gallery around the corner from his original showroom, both designed by Gerner Kronick + Valcarcel Architects. The boldness of the concept, a large, uninterrupted loft containing gallery, pantry and toilet, focuses on an orthogonal grid that is bisected by a metal and glass wall rotated seven inches off the grid, to provide intimate spaces for display. Lacking enclosed spaces, the staff creates rooms without walls by grouping furniture pieces as needed, demonstrating the versatility of modern design.

# Griswold, Heckel & Kelly Associates, Inc. and Space/Management Programs

GHK
55 West Wacker Drive
Suite 600
Chicago, IL 60601

Space/Management Programs
Suite 600
55 West Wacker Drive
Chicago, IL 60601

312.263.6605
312.263.1228 (Fax)
www.ghk.net

New York
Boston
Baltimore
Washington, DC

## Griswold, Heckel & Kelly Associates, Inc. and Space/Management Programs

## Huron Consulting Group LLC
## Chicago, Illinois

**Left:** Elevator lobby.

**Below:** Corridor and small meeting area.

**Lower left:** Informal conference room.

**Opposite:** Reception area.

**Photography:** Michael David Rose.

Talk about hitting the deck running. When former Arthur Andersen partners founded Huron Consulting Group LLC following the accounting giant's demise in 2002, the industry relationships sustained by such veterans as CEO Gary Holdren gave the fledgling provider of financial and operational consulting services excellent prospects for success. Sure enough, Huron has grown from some 250 consultants in a Chicago office to about 500 consultants in seven offices nationwide. As part of its ongoing service to Huron, Griswold Heckel & Kelly designed its new, 20,000 square foot Chicago headquarters to provide optimum working conditions for 80 employees in private offices, open work stations, and formal and informal conferencing spaces. The bright, spacious and functional environment features daylight, sweeping views and an impressive art collection that should take Huron's high achievers to new heights.

# Griswold, Heckel & Kelly Associates, Inc. and Space/Management Programs

Unilever ELT
Englewood, New Jersey

Unilever, one of the world's largest consumer products companies, has dramatically increased its involvement with consumers in the United States and Canada through its merger with Best Foods. Indeed, Unilever Bestfoods North America markets such well-known products as Lipton teas, Hellmann's mayonnaise, Ragú pasta sauces, Shedd's Country Crock spreads, Wish-Bone salad dressings, Knorr soups, Bertolli olive oil, Skippy peanut butter, and Lawry's seasonings. To support senior management of the newly formed Unilever North America after the merger, Griswold Heckel & Kelly has designed a 14,000-square foot facility for 17 members of the Executive Leadership Team (ELT) on the Unilever campus in Englewood, New Jersey. This high-powered work-place, featuring offices, reception area, lounges and executive pantry, enables Unilever executives to chart the direction of a company that employs over 15,200 people in 59 offices and manufacturing sites in 21 states in the United States and Puerto Rico, and some 2,400 people in 22 offices and manufacturing sites in six provinces in Canada.

Not coincidentally, it's also an appealing setting, appointed in hardwood veneers, stone, glass, drywall and modern furnishings, to enjoy Unilever's products first-hand.

**Above left:** Coffee bar.
**Top right:** Reception area.
**Above right:** Private office.
**Photography:** Peter Paige

# Griswold, Heckel & Kelly Associates, Inc. and Space/Management Programs

## Watson Wyatt Worldwide
## New York, New York

Advising businesses on human capital and financial management is a vital service with a venerable history at Watson Wyatt Worldwide, a global consulting firm with offices in the United Kingdom, North America, Europe, Latin America and Asia. After all, the company was formed in 1995 through the alliance of R Watson & Sons, a British actuarial firm founded in 1878, and The Wyatt Company, an American actuarial firm founded in 1946. Watson Wyatt's formidable management expertise was recently demonstrated during the relocation of its New York City office. Sensing an opportunity for change, the firm asked Griswold Heckel & Kelly to design the new, 85,000-square foot, three-story space for openness, outside views and illumination. The office focuses on the middle floor, where clients are received in such facilities as the reception area, conference rooms, video-conferencing room, hostess pantry and telephone breakout areas. Ample use of glass, limestone, carpet, textiles and color in key areas, the installation of reconfigurable spaces among the lower floor's workspaces, multipurpose meeting rooms and lunchroom, and the creation of a highly functional mail center and computer room make Watson Wyatt as up-to-date as its clients.

# Griswold, Heckel & Kelly Associates, Inc. and Space/Management Programs

## American Red Cross
## Washington, D.C.

**Below left:** Disaster operations center.
**Bottom left:** Encounter space.
**Below right:** Corridor.
**Bottom right:** Cafeteria.
**Photography:** Peter Paige.

Recent natural and man-made catastrophes keep the American Red Cross in the public eye and on the scene wherever need exists, causing the 1800-person staff at the new national headquarters in Washington, D.C. to make full use of the 500,000-square foot, 12-floor facility, designed by Griswold Heckel & Kelly Associates. Yet today's intense activity represents business as usual for the organization founded by Clara Barton in 1881. One of 175 National Societies supporting the global Red Cross Movement, the American Red Cross is independent of the federal government and serves victims at home and abroad. Its thoroughly modern facility includes offices, disaster operations center and such amenities as a cafeteria and fitness center. What makes the interiors particularly memorable is their way of combining effectiveness and economy with such whimsical touches as colorful graphics, canted and curving walls, and sophisticated lighting that people who face disasters and emergencies daily can appreciate.

# Griswold, Heckel & Kelly Associates, Inc.
# and Space/Management Programs

Quadriga
Chicago, Illinois

Describing itself as "The Future of Investing," Quadriga, a Superfund company, provides hedge funds for private investors around the world using highly secure trading environments that operate on a 24/7/365 basis. Investors would certainly be assured by the dynamic, new facility designed by Griswold Heckel & Kelly Associates for Quadriga executives and traders in Chicago. In the reception area, offices, conference rooms, trading room and cafe that constitute the 10,000-square foot, 1-level

space for 30 employees, the design team has created a lively, contemporary environment where state-of-the-art information technology is juxtaposed with exuberant posters and a majestic fish tank to help Quadriga employees stay alert and eager to make savvy in-

vestments. One sign of how well the scheme is working: Once the Chicago office was completed, Griswold Heckel & Kelly began work on another Quadriga office in New York.

## Griswold, Heckel & Kelly Associates, Inc. and Space/Management Programs

Constellation
Baltimore, Maryland

Since the relocation of Constellation's Baltimore headquarters occurred simultaneously with its reorganization, coordination, flexibility and agility were key to the design of the 66,300-square foot, three-floor facility for 190 employees by Griswold Heckel & Kelly. Constellation, a Fortune 500 energy company that is a leading supplier of electricity to large commercial and industrial customers as well as one of the nation's largest wholesale power sellers, and Baltimore Gas and Electric, a wholly owned utility distributing electricity and natural gas in central Maryland, worked closely together during the critical planning stages to

accommodate the new departmental structure. As a result, the entire, award-winning space—featuring a top floor for executives with a state-of-the-art, audio/visual boardroom—which is characterized by design solutions that cohesively tie all three floors together in a timeless, quiet elegance that should illuminate the company's image for years to come.

**Above:** Executive reception area.

**Left:** Boardroom.

**Photography:** Peter Paige

104

# H.Hendy Associates

4770 Campus Drive
Suite 100
Newport Beach, CA 92660
949.851.3080
949.851.0807 (Fax)
www.hhendy.com

## H.Hendy Associates

H.Hendy Associates
Newport Beach, California

Cultivating a team environment and creative problem solving was the key element in development of new offices for H.Hendy Associates. Some of the senior staff gave up enclosed, private offices in favor of "team rooms," which feature sit/stand work areas and pin-up walls, and are constantly in use for project management. The remaining private offices are a universal office solution, providing everyone with 10-feet X 15-feet and sliding glass-door entrances. In a notable departure from conventional office layouts

found in the design industry, H. Hendy created an open studio with a two-story skylight and library centrally located within natural traffic flow to further enhance cross-communication and -pollination of ideas among project teams. A project-process wall was designed with wall-talkers displaying various color boards and renderings of current projects to allow teams to collaborate and share. The open design tables have become the hub of activity and encourage creativity and problem-solving. To answer the challenge of maintaining

order in an area open to clients, Hendy utilized large lab trays common in research to accommodate projects-in-process. Herman Miller's Ethospace was selected to achieve maximum flexibility, including the addition of casters on all work surfaces and pedestals. An open and team-oriented environment is enhanced by selecting 54-inch high panels on the work

**Above Right:** Small conference room.

**Right:** Reception area.

**Above left:** Art Niche.

**Opposite:** Gallery corridor.

**Photography:** Milroy & Mc Aleer

# H.Hendy Associates

stations. The lunch room, placed on the interior window line, serves two purposes. At one end there is a periodical/research library fitted with comfortable leather seating and a European-height conference/coffee table, an area that is regularly utilized by the design staff for brainstorming sessions. The remainder of the space offers a pleasant retreat for lunch, impromptu staff meetings and vendor presentations, outfitted for flexibility with banquette seating along with the more traditional table and chairs. A refreshing color palette of aqua, chocolate and white is reflected in the reception area, which displays an espresso-stained zebra-wood and new Ward Bennett designed furniture by Geiger International. The main conference room features such touches as classic white Eames conference chairs around a Calcutta gold marble table. Suspended translucent panels in soft aqua add a touch of color and diffuse lighting to showcase client projects. Lighting is a key element in the design studio, where a combination of indirect, incandescent and fluorescent lighting, complemented by natural light from skylights, allows designers to view materials and finishes in the appropriate environment. Throughout the project, H.Hendy has demonstrated design innovation and a concern for practicality, blending materials ranging from exoticwoods, brick and marble, modular carpet, Chiliwich floor coverings and zolotone paint.

**Upper left:** Library.
**Upper right:** Large conference room.
**Left:** Lunchroom.
**Opposite:** Open design studio.

# H.Hendy Associates

A Major Financial Institution
Rolling Meadows, Illinois

**Top left and right:** Corridor and waiting area.

**Above:** Open office work area.

**Right:** Private offices.

**Opposite:** Reception.

**Photography:** Craig Dugan/ Hedrich Blessing.

For a financial institution with offices throughout the U.S., H. Hendy Associates was challenged to create a consistent identity that presents a sophisticated and substantial, yet not ostentatious, image. As important, the company needs to be viewed by its employees as successful and also as promoting creativity within a team-oriented environment. Adding to the challenge for the design team was the need to create office plans that are cost-effective and consistent to maximize economies of scale, yet are flexible enough to accommodate growth and allow customization of workstation standards to increase productivity. The client also required that the office designs be sensitive to the regional differences in areas in which it operates.

In approaching this assignment, H. Hendy developed company-wide standards for workstations, furniture and materials to meet the client's budgetary parameters. The team then utilized architectural and design features, such as varied wood tones and different color palettes, to achieve diversity in the office environment and to reflect regional differences. For example, a Midwestern location would feature darker woods and a more-subdued color scheme, while a West Coast office would include lighter woods and a more impactful color scheme.

**H.Hendy Associates**

A Major Financial Institution
Irvine, California

**Top left:** Reception.

**Above left:** Open workstations.

**Above right:** Conference room

**Right:** Lunchroom.

**Photography:** Scott McDonald/
Hedrich Blessing.

# Hellmuth, Obata + Kassabaum

620 Avenue of the Americas
6th Floor
New York, New York 10011
212.741.1200
212.633.1163 (Fax)
www.hokinteriors.com

**Below:** Corridor to cafe and conference center.

**Bottom, clockwise from upper left:** Reception lobby, researchers' open-plan work stations, boardroom, executive floor lounge.

**Opposite:** Atrium and communicating stair.

**Photography:** Ron Solomon.

# Hellmuth, Obata + Kassabaum

## MedImmune
## Gaithersburg, Maryland

The impressive, new, 210,000-square foot, five-story headquarters in Gaithersburg, Maryland for 600 employees of MedImmune, one of America's largest biotechnology companies, dramatically portrays the nature of leadership in biotechnology. MedImmune challenged Hellmuth, Obata + Kassabaum to create a project that would adapt to unpredictable growth and encourage interaction between researchers and other staff. To handle variable rates of growth, the floor plans consolidate common resources in core areas along major paths of travel, so offices can be distributed as blocks with minimal impact, and new buildings can be attached along established circulation routes. To stimulate contact and collaboration between researchers and their colleagues, the headquarters' atrium, cafe, library, conference rooms, and breakout spaces, occupy the intersection between the laboratory and administrative areas. These provisions along with shallow window-to-core depths, modular and flexible laboratory spaces, and a contemporary architectural image — should keep the 17-year-old company on its toes.

**Hellmuth, Obata + Kassabaum**

Ford Diesel
Dagenham, United Kingdom

Communication is key to the design of Ford Motor Company's new Diesel Design Centre in Dagenham, United Kingdom, and its impact can be felt as powerfully as the company's diesel engines throughout the interior of the 71,000 square foot 2-story wing, designed by Hellmuth, Obata + Kassabaum. As

an innovative building for the design and manufacture of diesel engines, the Centre combines the 700,000-square foot steel structure of a former vehicle plant, now remodeled for product development, testing and assembly, with a new 2-story wing, dedicated to reception, offices, meeting rooms, restaurant, and café.

The goal is to allow the Centre's 350 employees to share information and facilitate collaborative working in flexible groups within a clean, modern, high technology environment. The open-plan design of the new wing, for example, maintains uninterrupted vistas and increases face-to-face communication.

Office space is organized into team "neighborhoods" with fixed centers or hubs, occupied by administrative support staffs, which are aided by such accommodations as "support spines" enclosing meeting rooms, coffee bars and copy/ fax areas, fabric covered meeting pods for spontaneous work sessions,

and a restaurant café. Can better diesel technology and more satisfied customers be far behind?

**Above:** Conference room in support spine.

**Right:** Staff & visitor café.

**Far right:** Team neighborhood.

**Opposite above:** Reception.

**Opposite center left:** Informal meeting rooms / 'War' rooms.

**Opposite center right:** Staff & visitor restaurant.

**Design Team:** Aileen Asher, Sam Barker and Tim Eavis

**Photography:** Peter Cook, View

# Hellmuth, Obata + Kassabaum

Guy Carpenter
New York, New York

Two concerns were cited by reinsurance broker Guy Carpenter, a subsidiary of insurance brokerage Marsh & McLennan Companies, when they asked Hellmuth, Obata + Kassabaum to design their new New York headquarters. First, they wanted to create the right image for important client meetings. Second, they wanted to offer 350 headquarters employees an open and collaborative workplace that would not overwhelm them with sheer size--a 100,000-square foot floor plate. The design creates two decidedly different environments. The executive area, the setting for client functions, uses a formal corporate vocabulary of wood accents and a high percentage of private offices. By contrast, the general office area is populated by open-plan work stations and a limited number of enclosed offices, whose glass fronts give all employees access to natural light. As a means of establishing good spatial orientation in the general office area, the ceiling is

left exposed, except in conference rooms and private offices, and a curving "main street," sporting lively, printed, floating panels overhead, guides people through the office world of Guy Carpenter.

**Top Left:** Reception.

**Top:** Executive entry.

**Above left:** Community Center Conference.

**Above right:** Private offices.

**Opposite:** General office area.

**Photography:** Peter Paige.

**Hellmuth, Obata + Kassabaum**

Game Show Network
Santa Monica, California

**Above:** Executive lobby and executive conference room.

**Right:** Reception lobby/game area and main conference room.

**Far right:** Employee cafe.

**Photography:** Erich Koyama.

Game afficionados watch the Game Show Network, the only U.S. television network dedicated to game-related programming and interactive game playing, for many reasons. After all, the network jointly owned by Sony Pictures Entertainment and Liberty Media Corporation offers game shows, reality series, documentaries, video game programs, and casino games. However, when it was time for a new, 40,400-square foot, three-story facility in Santa Monica, designed by Hellmuth, Obata + Kassabaum, there was just one objective in mind: an effective workplace for 100 employees to help the network become bigger, better, and more popular. The design has resulted in a dramatic "rebranding" of an existing space to create private offices, conference rooms, game area, AVID bays/rooms, employee lunchroom and café, offering a largely open, whimsical and state-of-the-art environment praised by Brent Willman, the network's CFO, for being below budget, functional, "...plus it's fun!"

# JPC Architects

601 108th Avenue NE
Suite 2250
Bellevue, WA 98004
425.641.9200
425.637.8200 (Fax)
www.jpcarchitects.com

# JPC Architects

## Carney Badley Smith & Spellman
## Seattle, Washington

What a law office communicates to clients and staff is too important to ignore in today's pragmatic, cost-conscious and competitive business climate. So when Carney Badley Smith & Spellman, a Seattle, Washington law firm serving a diverse clientele ranging from individuals to large multi-national corporations, approached JPC Architects to design its new, 19,000-square foot, single-floor, 80-person office, the firm's design committee called for a significant departure from its existing "opulent '80s" facility. Not only did the attorneys request a substantial reduction in total floor area, they wanted to relocate staff from two existing floors in one downtown office tower to one floor in a less costly location. The new office succeeds in projecting a highly positive image. Floor area has been reduced 25 percent by dropping lawyers' offices to 150 square feet apiece—the same for partners and associates—and shedding most of their space-consuming law books in the face of overwhelming reliance on computerized data bases and the Internet for research. The new environment strikes a bold, progressive posture through the use of more color, less wood and unique, sculptural shapes that give the interior architecture a sophisticated character all its own. Visitors notice the difference as soon as they enter the rotunda-like reception area that serves as the focal point for the entire floor plan. For the employees, who include such distinguished legal practitioners as John Spellman, former Governor of the State of Washington, the new office helps them share their clients' prevailing view of the world.

**Above left:** Reception area seating.

**Above:** View from reception area to conference room.

**Top:** Typical corridor.

**Opposite:** Elevator lobby and reception area.

**Photography:** Fred Housel.

# JPC Architects

## SS+K
## Bellevue, Washington

**Right:** Visitors' seating within reception area.

**Below:** Conference room with sliding doors retracted.

**Opposite:** View of reception area from reception desk.

**Photography:** Ben Benschneider.

Eager to express its creative and collaborative culture in a new, 5,000-square foot, 20-person office in Bellevue, Washington, Shepardson, Stern + Kaminsky or SS+K, a New York-based public relations and marketing firm founded in 1993. SS+K who serves such clients as Time Warner, Blue Cross/Blue Shield and Nike, asked JPC Architects for a facility that would link the formal activity of the reception area with the creative energy of the main studio. The architect met this challenge with a light, airy and dynamic design that minimizes the number of private offices and locates most of them in the interior of the building. Not only does the facility give the open studio landscape the benefit of outdoor views and natural light, it applies intense color to strategic accent walls for dramatic impact. To spread the excitement of the creative process beyond the main studio, the reception area is configured as a dual purpose space. Guests arriving at the office are graciously and comfortably accommodated with lounge seating. In addition, SS+K project teams can enjoy the lounge seating for teaming sessions and take advantage of the adjacent conference room with its large retractable sliding glass doors. Either way, the urge to roll up your sleeves and brainstorm is almost irresistible.

**JPC Architects**

Corbis
Seattle, Washington

No one has a monopoly on the world's visual images, but a good place to initiate any search would be Corbis, one of the world's leading providers of licensed images for advertising, books, newspapers, magazines, TV and film. Established by Microsoft co-founder Bill Gates in 1989, Corbis became widely known through its 1995 acquisition of the Bettmann Archive, the renowned collection of 20th century historical imagery created by Dr. Otto Bettmann. The new, 73,631-square foot, five-level, 300-person headquarters of Corbis, designed by JPC Architects, is located in a historic Seattle bank building where it projects an appropriately photogenic image. The sleek, high-tech facility, which encompasses open and private offices, conference areas, lunch room, data center, video laboratories and archive, combines respect for its historic surroundings with forward thinking about technology by playing its contemporary furnishings off the building's existing classic historical forms and the massive seismic retrofitted structure of large-diameter black steel pipes. High walls of translucent panels define a main path and small-scale work environments within a three-and-one-half story atrium that includes a mezzanine and an interior verandah at the rear of the main space that serves as a primary teaming spot. With even the bank vault saved for re-use by Corbis, the former bank is a bank once more—safeguarding digital-age assets.

**Above:** Entrance lobby.

**Opposite above left:** Reception area.

**Opposite below left:** Central common area.

**Opposite below right:** Remodeled bank vault.

**Photography:** Ben Benschneider.

**JPC Architects**

OppenheimerFunds Services
Bellevue, Washington

How do you make clients feel welcome beyond the reception area of an office, where dimensions and budgets are typically more generous? For Oppenheimer-Funds Services, the arm of OppenheimerFunds that provides investment management services to investors and their financial advisors, the need for a client-friendly environment for its new, 20,000-square foot, 80-person Bellevue, Washington office would indeed extend into its back office areas. JPC Architects' shrewd use of colors, finishes, indirect and natural lighting radiate a strong sense of warmth and spaciousness, taking the edge off a typical gray Northwest winter day. Whether clients happen to be visiting private offices, sitting in conference rooms or passing open work stations, they will find a warm greeting.

**Above:** Reception area.
**Left:** Open plan work stations.
**Below:** Private office.
**Photography:** Ben Benschneider.

# Leotta Designers Inc.

601 Brickell Key Drive
Suite 602
Miami, FL 33131
305.371.4949
305.371.2844 (Fax)
www.leottadesigners.com

Leotta Designers Inc.

**Leotta Designers Inc.**  Major International Private Bank
Miami, Florida

**Top:** Reception.
**Above:** Executive corridor.
**Right:** Back office.
**Opposite:** Client meeting room.
**Photography:** Joseph Lapeyra.

If Spanish is Miami's lingua franca, that's fine with the financial institutions doing business in toney Brickell Avenue or bustling Downtown Miami. Florida's most populated city—362,000 residents in a metropolitan region of 2,253,000—is the U.S. gateway to Latin America. While such neighbors as Miami Beach and Coconut Grove boast greater tourist appeal, Miami is where business leaders meet, get acquainted and consummate deals. Thus, a Major International Private Bank commissioned Leotta

Designers to design and later expand an 8,000-square foot office for 35 employees as a dignified yet economical setting to receive clients. The recently completed facility, comprising reception, private offices, clerical area, conference rooms, private banking room, teller room, and copy and supply room, succeeds by concentrating high-end materials like stone and wood in client areas. In this way, interior design resembles real estate development, focusing on location, location, location.

# Leotta Designers Inc.

Credit Suisse
Miami, Florida

**Top:** Small client meeting room.
**Above:** Reception.
**Right:** Family meeting room.
**Opposite:** View from reception to conference room.
**Photography:** Nancy Watson.

Zurich-based Credit Suisse, the global provider of financial services is conducting a major drive to market private banking and financial advisory services and banking products to private clients in Latin America. When it asked Leotta Designers to design its new, 5,381-square foot Representative Office for 18 employees in the city's prestigious Brickell Avenue corridor, it requested a client-focused and sophisticated environment to convey visitors from a dramatic front entry and reception area to surrounding conference rooms of varying size and formality. What visitors don't see, however, are the problems that arose from large columns in the reception area and a combination of angled and curved perimeter walls that trace the building's distinctive facades. These obstacles have been so skillfully incorporated in the design that visitors regularly compliment Credit Suisse on its new sleek offices. Who would suppose that the intriguing geometry of the reception area is a solution for angled walls as well as innovative architecture?

# Leotta Designers Inc.

## Dade Paper Co.
## Miami, Florida

Headquarters and interiors like the new, 222,000-square foot, two-story facility in Miami designed by Leotta Designers for Dade Paper Co. do not represent your standard formula design. Founded in 1939, Dade Paper is the foremost supplier of premium paper, plastic and foam disposables, as well as janitorial/sanitation supplies and equipment, in the southeastern United States, Puerto Rico and the Caribbean. Its headquarters consists of a 125-person office and 100-person warehouse occupying the same, new, freestanding structure, and its dual nature presented the design team with the challenge of fitting the company's demanding building program requirements into two distinct halves of a structure that could be regarded as a major core and tower element bisecting a rectangle. Needless to say, the building program covered a wide range of activities, including reception, executive suite, product presentation room, conference rooms, private offices, break area, washrooms, kitchens, customer service and Will Call Center. The design solution succeeds by drawing on a flexible space plan and a comprehensive vocabulary of materials and furnishings that were specially created to satisfy multiple functions and departments with unique spatial requirements, including the Will Call Center. In fact, the un-conventional facility has far exceeded Dade Paper's expectations for its new home.

**Above:** Executive office.

**Left:** Executive conference room.

**Below:** Executive suite.

**Opposite:** Reception.

**Photography:** Nancy Watson, and Joe Lapeyra (opposite page).

# Leotta Designers Inc.

**Above:** Will Call Center.

**Below left:** Product presentation room.

**Photography:** Nancy Watson.

# Mancini • Duffy

39 West 13th Street
New York, NY 10011
212.938.1260
800.298.0868
212.938.1267 (Fax)
www.manciniduffy.com
info@manciniduffy.com

New York
New Jersey
Connecticut
California
Washington DC
London UK

**Mancini•Duffy**

Ritz-Carlton Hotel Company
Chevy Chase, MD

Guests of The Ritz-Carlton hotels and resorts, a chain of 58 luxury hotels worldwide renowned for sumptuous surroundings and legendary service, would be pleased to check into the new, 40,500-square-foot, two-level, 120-person headquarters for the Ritz-Carlton Hotel Company in Chevy Chase, Maryland, designed by Mancini•Duffy. And why not? The award-winning facility, encompassing reception area, open and private offices, conference rooms, lounge and central stair, acts as a visual affirmation of the Ritz-Carlton brand as well as a support facility for the worldwide network of hotels it serves. As such, the workplace gives the organization the opportunity to describe itself in more contemporary terms, combining modern architectural forms with traditional interior appointments, even as it provides an effective and pleasant environment for the staff. Evidence of the design's care and thoughtfulness are everywhere. When visitors arrive at the reception area, for example, they can proceed directly to the adjacent boardroom and conference center. In addition, offices are structured as flexible, cellular units to facilitate change, open workstations line the perimeter to maximize daylight and views, the lounge serves as a multi-function space for formal and informal events, and the central stair adds drama and convenience, rising to a casual gathering space and espresso/coffee pantry that add a touch of Ritz-Carlton to the workday.

**Above:** Reception.

**Right:** Connecting stair.

**Opposite above:** Conference room.

**Opposite below:** Breakout.

**Photography:** Peter Paige.

**Mancini•Duffy**

Reed Elsevier
New York, New York

Decision makers in 23 business sectors rely on the more than 130 publications and 115 websites of Reed Business Information, making this U.S. subsidiary of Reed Elsevier Group, the Anglo-Dutch global media powerhouse, North America's largest B2B publisher. Similarly, scientists read over 1,200 scientific journals from Elsevier Science, making this subsidiary of Reed Elsevier the world's leading publisher of scientific journals. The compatible yet different personalities of the two companies are evident in the new, 450,000-square-foot, 15-level, 500-person headquarters they share in New York, designed by Mancini•Duffy, which consolidates business units from seven locations throughout Manhattan. While the cost-effective construction is based on universal planning, the design emphasizes corporate identity and division branding. Consequently, Elsevier Science's workplace is more hierarchical with perimeter private offices, while Reed Business locates open work-stations on the perimeter to share daylight, though both have reception areas, lounges, conference rooms and employee cafés. Either way, this award-winning facility works.

**Above:** Reception.

**Left:** Workstations.

**Far left:** Executive conference room.

**Photography:** Peter Paige.

**Mancini•Duffy**    EMI Recorded Music
New York, New York

No matter what music you enjoy, chances are some of the approximately 1,000 artists on EMI Recorded Music's 70-plus labels are on your playlists. Whether the artist is the Beastie Boys on Capitol Records performing "Ch-Check It Out" or Stephen Cleobury on EMI Classics conducting Rachmaninov's Liturgy of St. John Chrysostom, it's all music to the ears at EMI's new, 150,000-square-foot, 10-story (plus roof garden) New York office, 150 Fifth Avenue. The land-marked building, acquired by EMI Recorded Music as North American headquar-ters for itself, parent compa-ny EMI Group, Virgin Records, and the New York office of Capitol Records, houses some 400 employees in a facility designed by Mancini•Duffy with reception areas, open-plan and private offices, conference rooms, lounges, employee cafeteria and roof garden. Though the project's 16-week schedule was tight, the handsome, award-winning design cleverly combines old and new to preserve the build-ing's Romanesque flavor and give each division a visual personality to accompany its own, unique sound.

**Above left:** Capitol Records reception.

**Above right:** Emloyee lounge.

**Top right:** Workstations.

**Photography:** Peter Paige.

## Mancini•Duffy  Time Warner Center
New York, New York

**Right:** Executive boardroom corridor.

**Bottom right:** Cafeteria.

**Below:** Interior staircase.

**Opposite:** Boardroom complex breakout.

**Photography:** Peter Paige.

In one of New York's major corporate moves, Time Warner has relocated its headquarters from fabled Rockefeller Center to spacious Columbus Circle. The giant media company's new, 350,000-square foot, 17-story space at Time Warner Center, designed by Perkins & Will in collaboration with Mancini•Duffy, fully exploits the new, 865,000-square-foot Time Warner Center and the location's proximity to Central Park to give some 1,600 employees an extraordinary environment for general and executive offices and such amenities as a cafeteria, executive dining rooms, screening theater complex, boardroom and associated pre-function area, and training rooms. Not only are natural light and spectacular views visible everywhere, employees and visitors have the benefit of a state-of-the-art wireless-G network, and voice-over IP communication, audio-visual and distributed media systems, all discreetly integrated with interiors of fine hardwoods, clear and patterned glass, brushed and polished stainless steel, terrazzo, glass mosaic tile, carpet and encaustic paint. A new era has dawned for Time Warner and Columbus Circle.

142

The power of a lobby renovation radiates from Mancini•Duffy's work at New York's 1250 Broadway. When real estate investor S.L. Green acquired the high-visibility property in the Greeley Square neighborhood, it was an undistinguished, Class B building. The new, expanded lobby incorporates a frameless glass facade to admit more natural light, raises the ceiling to match an exterior colonnade, installs a wall-mounted illuminated glass box to advertise the address, and adds a sundries store and stylish concierge desk. New tenants are taking notice—and signing leases.

**Above:** Lobby exterior.
**Right:** Reception desk.
**Photography:** Michael Moran.

# Margulies & Associates

234 Congress Street
Boston, MA 02110
617.482.3232
617.482.0374 (Fax)
www.margulies.com

## Margulies & Associates

Payton Construction
Headquarters
Boston, Massachusetts

Founded in 1986 to provide construction services to owners and architects, Payton Construction encouraged Margulies & Associates to design a fascinating new headquarters where the building's idiosyncrasies are transformed into focal points. The 40,000 square feet of office space straddled two recently connected former mill buildings, so floor levels didn't align and structural grids didn't match. Instead of trying to camouflage the discontinuity of the space, Margulies & Associates created an interesting focal point by carving out an eight-foot corridor to serve as an internal "street". Bordered by non-parallel walls, the corridor incorporates irregular floor patterns and expressive ceiling elements to create interesting but discrete spaces for gathering throughout the passage. Broken up and interrupted with angled mast-like pillars, the sail-shaped soffits enhance the intersection of the main hallway with the side corridors. To reflect the office's proximity to Boston Harbor, Margulies & Associates chose a blue and gray color scheme and introduced curving lines, fixtures and furniture reminiscent of rippling waves. William Payton happily observes, "The resulting space is truly inspirational."

**Right:** Boardroom.

**Below left:** Open plan area.

**Below right:** Reception.

**Opposite:** Corridor.

**Photography:** Warren Patterson

**Margulies & Associates**

JAFCO Ventures
Waltham, Massachusetts

**Above left:** Reception.

**Above right:** Corridor.

**Left:** Private offices seen through conference room.

**Far left:** Conference room.

**Photography:** Warren Patterson.

Driven by a mission to invest in top-tier emerging companies in the U.S., and to connect portfolio companies with business opportunities in Asia, JAFCO's 5,000-square foot, 15-person offices required a sophisticated, subtle approach to support the work of its team of international investors. Magnificent views of the Cambridge Reservoir and downtown Boston greet staff and visitors as they enter the long and thin space, defined by windowed private offices. To add interest to the linear layout, the designers of Margulies & Associates introduced an undulating wall of cherry wood "fins," stainless steel hardware and floor-to-ceiling glass. When viewed at an angle, the "fins" create a Venetian-blind-like effect, providing a sense of scale for the corridor, as well as partial privacy for the office occupants. "We were searching for a design statement to reflect our focus on the collaborative nature of our investment approach," explained Chuan Thor, Partner. Inspired by the transparency of the spacious private offices and convenient conference facilities, JAFCO's venture capital partners are working together to forge new connections between the United States and Asia.

## Margulies & Associates

## Intercontinental Real Estate Corporation
## Boston, Massachusetts

**Below left:** Exterior.

**Below right:** Conference rooms.

**Bottom:** Informal conference room surrounded by office area.

**Opposite:** Atrium.

**Photography:** Warren Patterson.

With just 13,400 square feet of allowable building space on a highly visible site along the Charles River in Boston, Intercontinental Real Estate Corporation, a real estate investment and management company, turned to Margulies & Associates for a high-profile design solution for the company's world headquarters. To meet Intercontinental's goal of increasing internal collaboration in a spacious environment filled with natural light, Margulies & Associates designed private and open offices, conference rooms, a dining area and a kitchen around an airy enclosed atrium. A distinctive glass tower leads to a roof deck with views of the Boston skyline, while glass-walled conference rooms overlook parks bordering the Charles River. A brise-soleil accentuates the building's roofline and

provides solar shading to mitigate the glare which might otherwise be associated with extensive glazing. The lighting design provides dramatic accent for the contemporary art collection and enhances the reflective and transparent qualities of the building at night, showcasing the company's commitment to quality development and construction. Notes Paul Palandjian, Intercontinental's president, "Visitors never fail to be awed by the quality of the space that we now enjoy."

## Margulies & Associates

## Barefoot Books
## Cambridge, Massachusetts

Characterized by rich illustrations and multi-cultural themes, the covers of its books reflect the distinctive personality of Barefoot Books, a growing children's book publisher. For its corporate headquarters in Cambridge, Massachusetts, Barefoot Books wanted bright, expressive and unusual office space. "Our books are all about color and style, and the space we work in has to reflect that," Nancy Traversy, president of Barefoot Books, said in a recent article in *The Wall Street Journal.* Margulies & Associates conceived a system of freestanding dividers to partition the large, open areas of the former warehouse building into work zones and functional areas. Retaining many existing building components including walls, finishes and lighting, the design team added inexpensive new materials and finishes to achieve the maximum visual effect from a modest budget. Since the high ceiling was unsuitable for a dropped ceiling treatment, building service housings were carefully located and stacked to reduce their presence. The attractive result is as light-hearted as it is functional.

**Above:** Views showing the freestanding dividers.

**Photography:** Warren Patterson.

# McCarthy Nordburg

3333 E. Camelback Road
Suite 180
Phoenix, AZ 85018
602.955.4499
602.955.4599 (Fax)
www.mccarthynordburg.com

## McCarthy Nordburg

### Discount Tire Company
### Scottsdale, Arizona

A 157,000-square foot, two-story, 600-person facility represents a large interior space by any measure, and the new Scottsdale, Arizona headquarters of Discount Tire Company, America's largest independent tire dealer with 8,415 employees working at 528 stores, 19 warehouses, 19 regional offices and five regional distribution centers serving stores in 18 states, is no exception. However, employees and visitors in Discount Tire's home office, designed by McCarthy Nordburg, encounter an environment that feels far more intimate, attractive and supportive than its

sheer size would suggest. Why? In accommodating the business founded in 1960 by owner Bruce Halle, the architect has created a design that provides appropriately scaled rooms for a range of activities, subtly integrates employee amenities—including an extensive corporate art collection with light-sensitive antique posters—into the overall interior scheme, and establishes a gracious public image with a lobby that deliberately evokes a resort hotel. Thus, the private and open offices, board room, conference rooms, lunch room and fitness center help make each working day at head-quarters as productive as Discount Tire's far-flung wholesale and retail operations.

**Above:** Reception lobby.
**Left:** Executive lounge.
**Far left:** Lunch room.
**Opposite:** Board room.
**Photography:** Michael Norton.

**McCarthy Nordburg**

Harris Trust at the Biltmore
Phoenix, Arizona

Doing business on the ground floor of an office building in a fashionable part of Phoenix, just a short drive from the legendary Arizona Biltmore Resort and Spa, the new, 5,000-square foot branch of Harris Trust Bank of Arizona takes care to dress properly for the occasion. The award-winning design by McCarthy Nordburg for Harris Bank, encompassing the lobby, teller line, check center, sales area and private administrative offices, reflects the affluence of the community with fine furnishings placed in an architectural setting of slate, granite, marble and maple wood. The overall effect conveys a strong sense of financial security and success, aided by skillful use of the building's 15-foot high ceiling, and such attentive details as a touch-down area where customers can watch the news before heading to work or play.

# McCarthy Nordburg

Gust Rosenfeld
Phoenix, Arizona

Highly esteemed organizations typically treat all their personnel with respect, as the law firm of Gust Rosenfeld demonstrates at its new, 28,200-square foot, two-level, 105-person Phoenix office, designed by McCarthy Nordburg. A law firm founded in 1921 that provides legal advice, creative insights and practical solutions in all areas of business, public and civil law, Gust Rosenfeld wanted to simultaneously locate all attorneys' private offices along the building's exterior and share natural light from the periphery with employees in the interior.

McCarthy Nordburg's fresh, contemporary design satisfies that objective with clerestory windows in the corridor walls of private offices, and adds other interesting design details such as canted horizontal surfaces that discourage random paper placement, teamed with built-in in/out boxes and other custom-designed storage units, a large and impressive law library, and the handsome installation of the firm's historic regional photography collection. No matter where Gust Rosenfeld's employees are, in private offices, administrative

work stations, conference rooms, library, lunchroom or reception area, a consistently functional and appealing environment is present to support them.

**Right:** Main conference room.

**Below:** Reception area.

**Opposite below left:** Conference room.

**Opposite below center:** Corridor with custom storage units.

**Photography:** Michael Norton.

## McCarthy Nordburg

## Ottawa University
## Phoenix, Arizona

Can a comprehensive, not-for-profit educational institution affiliated with the American Baptist Churches be nurturing academic offspring over a century after its founding in 1865? For Ottawa University, which maintains a residential campus in Ottawa, Kansas and adult campuses in Kansas, Arizona, Wisconsin, Indiana and Missouri, along with international instructional sites in Hong Kong, Singapore and Malaysia, the question is timely--because the school has not stopped growing. In fact, a new, 40,000-square foot, two-story administrative building, featuring interior architecture by McCarthy Nordburg, opened as part of the February 20, 2004 inauguration of Ottawa's newest campus in Phoenix, providing students larger classrooms, ample parking space and an increasingly constructive, educational environment. The objective for the facility, which includes staff and faculty offices, conference rooms, break rooms, a classroom and student services, was to provide a professional image of administrative control that retained a student-oriented and warm atmosphere. Judging from the response on campus, the new building is making the grade.

**Left:** Entrance lobby from balcony.

**Above right:** Entrance lobby and balcony.

**Right:** Stairwell and main corridor.

**Photography:** Michael Norton.

# Meyer Associates, Inc.

227 East Lancaster Avenue
Ardmore, PA 19003
610.649.8500
610.649.8509 (Fax)
www.meyer-associates.com

**Meyer Associates, Inc.**

Analytical Graphics, Inc.
Exton, Pennsylvania

**Top left:** Reception.

**Above left:** Dining area with servery.

**Above center:** "Water cooler" collaborative area.

**Above right:** Boardroom with custom video conference table.

**Photography:** Don Pearse.

Enjoying strong growth throughout its 15-year history, Analytical Graphics, a provider of commercial off-the-shelf analysis and visualization software to more than 30,000 aerospace, defense, and intelligence professionals worldwide, is also known as an out- standing and progressive employer. To reinforce the efforts of its employees in providing quality products and services, and to ensure that its workplace reflects its corporate culture, the company recently asked Meyer Associates to design a new, 66,200- square foot, three-level office in suburban Philadelphia. As a result, floor plans incorporate a constellation-like layout with circular brainstorming rooms set throughout the open-plan spaces, along with other expressions of the circular motif and a striking, aerodynamic "wing wall" at the reception area, to create a dramatic and stimulating workplace. In addition, such amenities as a kitchen/servery, fitness room with lockers and showers, laundry, lunchroom with fireplace, and children's room, assisting parents whose children are sick or off from school, make this attractive, functional and technologically advanced open office envi- ronment a most satisfying place to work.

# Meyer Associates, Inc.

## American College of Radiology
## Philadelphia, Pennsylvania

**Above left:** Reception.

**Above right:** Teaming area.

**Left:** Seating area looking into computer room.

**Opposite:** Boardroom.

**Photography:** Don Pearse.

It's not obvious to a visitor that the clinical research division of the American College of Radiology launched a major reorganization with the opening of its new, 87,000-square foot Philadelphia office. However, it has successfully refocused from individual departments to interdepartmental teams despite initial resistance from employees, and the new space has helped make it happen. How did this clinical research division devoted to cancer research rally employees around the change? Much credit goes to direct personnel involvement. Yet the new office, designed by Meyer Associates, is another source of satisfaction for the work force, because it meets basic needs in forthright and creative ways. Employees at all open-plan work stations enjoy daylight, for example, thanks to expansive perimeter windows and skillful furniture layouts, as well as privacy, through special retreat rooms. Both team and individual areas are attractively outfitted with good lighting and appropriate furnishings. Special design details, such as exposed ceilings, cherry wood veneering, and well-placed color accents, add interest at little cost. The computer room is showcased for visitors because data is at the heart of it's research. Employees and visitors concur: What's not to like?

## Meyer Associates, Inc.

Berwind Property Group
Philadelphia, Pennsylvania

Emulating parents can motivate businesses as well as individuals, as Berwind Property Group, Ltd. demonstrates in its newly remodeled, 30,000-square foot, single-floor Philadelphia headquarters for 100 employees, designed by Meyer Associates. Since the distinguished headquarters of parent company Berwind Corporation occupies the same building, Berwind Property Group sought to attain the same, high quality in its own office. In fact, the makeover of the existing premises for the real estate operator, which is active in property acquisition, development and investment management nationwide, has dramatically improved its perimeter offices and open administrative work areas. Besides installing floor-to-ceiling glazing to transmit daylight and views from private offices to the interior, creating artwork niches at the ends of long corridors as focal points, and concealing copy/mail areas behind administrative stations, the interiors bring a progressive European sophistication to the space. For a company founded in 1980, it's an impressive tribute to a parent founded in 1886.

**Above:** Reception.

**Right:** Conference room.

**Opposite above:** Corridor with artwork niche.

**Opposite below:** Small conference room.

**Photography:** Don Pearse.

**Mojo • Stumer Associates, P.C.**

Bank of Smithtown
Wading River, New York

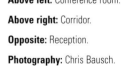

**Above left:** Conference room.
**Above right:** Corridor.
**Opposite:** Reception.
**Photography:** Chris Bausch.

Is there a bank where customers sit in club chairs to discuss their finances with bankers stationed at desks on the banking floor, batteries of television monitors provide information on banking products and services, and a standard teller counter is nowhere to be found? For customers at the handsome, new, 4,200-square foot Wading River, New York office of Bank of Smithtown, designed by Mojo-Stumer Associates, the philosophy of "one-to-one" personal service has been made dramatically visible and effective. Now in its 95th year as an independent bank offering a complete range of commercial and consumer banking services, Bank of Smithtown has made a reputation for celebrating its historic legacy while acting like a much younger institution. Indeed, the Bank's willingness to please customers has inspired it to provide the latest in financial products and services, backed by state-of-the-art technology and contemporary facilities such as the Wading River office. The building program for this location, which encompasses private offices, a conference room, a back office and a lunch room in addition to a banking floor, places all of its activities on a single floor, and signals changes of function through a beautifully detailed composition of curving walls, ceilings and floors. Does this determined outreach to

# Mojo • Stumer Associates, P.C.

customers pay off for the Bank? Consider that the Bank's stock price has grown steadily over the last decade, rising from $3.08 in 1994 to $45.75 in 2003. Or the fact that the Bank, whose assets currently stand at over $565 million, reported a net income in 2003 of $9.1 million, reflecting a robust return on equity of 24.74 percent and a respectable return on assets of 1.8 percent. Or the Bank's decision to design, build and operate seven more branch banks in the same image of Venetian plaster, upholstered walls, carpet with graphics, stone and wood floors, metal ceilings and fine furnishings. For customers of Bank of Smithtown, the future is right on schedule.

**Above:** Lunch room.

**Opposite:** Architectural detail.

# Mojo • Stumer Associates, P.C.

Mojo • Stumer Associates
Greenvale, New York

**Below:** Entrance and reception.
**Right:** View from entrance.
**Photography:** Phil Ennis.

The moment you enter the new, 8,000-square foot, one-level office, designed by Mojo-Stumer Associates in Greenvale, New York to house its own staff of 30 employees, you immediately sense this is not your prototypical architecture studio. An architect usually covers every available wall with photographs and renderings of his or her work that complement scale models scattered throughout the facility. Here, you will find no pictures on any wall. The clean, elegant and meticulously detailed forms of the walls, ceilings and floors create a spacious, subtly illuminated and clearly defined environment that expresses the firm's mission, "Improving the quality of our clients' lives through better and more creative architecture." The construction, which consists of slate, cold-rolled steel and other metals, etched glass, lacquer, ash and maple and uses soft, muted colors, is no less satisfying despite being subjected to rigorous tests of time, budget and function. Yet it has produced a satisfying workplace that includes a reception area, conference room, two studios (one apiece for architecture and interior design), library, private offices and file space. Why shouldn't the award-

# Mojo • Stumer Associates, P.C.

winning work of a firm founded in 1980 by Thomas Mojo, AIA, Mark Stumer, AIA, and respected for its honest, handsome and practical design for residential, office, leisure and retail clients, be enjoyed by the people who create it? For the staff of Mojo-Stumer, the new facility literally brings good design home.

**Left:** Corridor.
**Bottom:** Studio.

# NBBJ

Beijing
Columbus
London
Los Angeles
New York
San Francisco
Seattle

www.nbbj.com

NBBJ

# NBBJ

## Starbucks
## Seattle, Washington

**Below left:** Communicating stair and poster display.

**Below right:** Meeting areas, including central commons.

**Opposite:** Coffee roaster, café.

**Photography:** Paul Warchol and Steve Dubinsky.

Enjoying a cup of coffee has never been the same since Howard Schultz joined Seattle coffee brewer and retailer, Starbucks, in 1982. Thirteen years after the company opened its first location in Seattle, Schultz persuaded the company to test a European-style coffee bar. Now, after the opening of over 8,000 stores and numerous innovations such as on-site wireless Internet access, the "Starbucks experience" is a global phenomenon. It is backed by a new, one-million-square-foot Seattle headquarters designed by NBBJ for 1,000 people through the adaptive reuse of a Sears warehouse. To accommodate unusually high growth (about 35% per year), the new space required flexibility with options to expand. Shultz's vision was to create a positive, stimulating environment that fosters democratic principles and informal gatherings—much like the communicative atmosphere found in the stores. The designers mixed departments by floor to stimulate interaction and created a central commons for spontaneous gatherings. Throughout the space, posters display the new marketing materials, coffee plants grow in pots and, in the top floor commons area, an antique coffee roaster, retrofitted with modern technology, is used for demonstrations and sample batches—all to tie the company more closely to the coffee bean. The new workplace supports Starbuck's passion for customer service, global citizenship and community investment.

# NBBJ-HUS-PKA

## Telenor
## Fornebu, Norway

**Below:** Main circulation spine with views of plaza and fjord.

**Bottom:** Typical wireless, paper-less work area.

**Right:** Atrium with café.

**Opposite:** One of Telenor's four restaurants.

**Photography:** Tim Griffith and Christian Richters.

A runway at the former Olso International Airport is the site of a new 137,000-square-meter headquarters that charts the transformation of Telenor from Norweigan Telecom, a state monopoly, to a public corporation and a partly privatized company listed on the stock exchange. Today Telenor is a dynamic organization that maintains its leading position through its cutting edge expertise. The high-tech headquarters, designed by NBBJ-HUS-PKA and Dark Design to consoli-date over 7,000 employees at 6,000 workstations, helps Telenor transform the way it conducts business by unifying the company and encouraging collaboration. Because of the volatility of the telecommuni-cations industry, Telenor Fornebu was designed with flexibility in mind. Eight office wings and atriums organize the headquarters into work units of 30 to 40 people. Equipped with cell phones and laptops, employees share the communal desks, which can be raised and lowered. Glassed-in rooms provide privacy when needed.

Connecting the atriums are two indoor "boulevards" that run the length of the building. Like all the public space shared by employees, they are designed to en-courage informal sharing of information. To allow for this, 225 meeting rooms of various sizes are located throughout the building. And because no-one is tied to a desk by a computer or phone line, people tend to be out and about more.

New York Tolerance Center
New York, New York

As difficult as it may be to admit, man's inhumanity to man still claims innocent victims in the 21st century. The urgency of the matter helps explain why the Simon Wiesenthal Center, a Los Angeles-based international Jewish human rights organization dedicated to preserving the memory of the Holocaust, has established the new, 20,000-square-foot New York Tolerance Center, designed by NBBJ. To help companies, educators, law enforcement officials and government representatives explore issues of diversity, prejudice, tolerance, and cooperation in the workplace and community, the Center offers interactive workshops, exhibits and videos modeled along the successful Tools for Tolerance Program in Los Angeles. The spaces are designed to envelope the audience, starting with the screening room theater and pre-function space on the first floor and continuing to the lower level concourse of exhibits, classrooms and administrative areas. It's an immersion visitors are unlikely to forget.

**Above left:** Entrance lobby.

**Above right:** Concourse of exhibits.

**Opposite:** Smart Wall.

**Photography:** Michael Moran.

Amgen is a company at the forefront of change in the biotech market. As the nature of research shifts, they are faced with critical questions. How do they meld their research culture with the need to think like manufacturers? How do they blend the culture of research scientists with the culture of business? Approaching these issues head on with its new headquarters, Amgen looked to NBBJ to create an architectural framework for the office suites and labs that adapts to the changing nature of the organization. Scientists by nature are curious. The process of research and discovery leads them down roads they had no idea they would travel. Amgen's new, 29-acre campus on Seattle's Elliott Bay consolidates staff who were previously at nine different locations and embraces a simple premise: support this curiosity and create a dynamic environment for scientific interaction, information exchange and organizational identity.

**Above left:** Hallway with artwork.

**Above right:** Internal "helix" stair.

**Right:** Staff café.

**Photography:** Christian Richters.

# NELSON

222-30 Walnut Street
Philadelphia, PA 19106
215.925.6562
215.925.9151 (Fax)
www.nelsononline.com

NELSON

# NELSON

## Wachovia Calibre
## Winston Salem, North Carolina

**Below left:** Entry to open plan space.

**Right:** Customer reception.

**Bottom:** Open plan operations.

**Photography:** Mark Henninger, Imagic Digital.

Families with multi-generational wealth have unique financial needs, and Calibre, a Wachovia Corporation subsidiary, wants to acquaint them with its distinctive blend of asset strategy and investment management, financial and tax planning, fiduciary and estate administration, banking and credit services, charitable services, and investment custodial services. For this reason, Calibre's 10,000-square foot, one-floor office for 35 employees in Winston Salem, North Carolina has been designed by NELSON to welcome clients to a sophisticated, collegial environment of trust, expertise and experience. The facility, which includes conference rooms, reception and surrounding waiting areas for customers, along with private offices, open plan work stations, break room and private restrooms, directs clients along a main corridor, where receptions can be held when all meeting spaces are opened up, to private spaces where Calibre officers welcome them. Every detail, from multi-level ceilings, indirect lighting, hardwood veneers, stone and brushed stainless steel to transitional furniture and antiques, reveals a world of dedicated professional service.

**NELSON**

Hudson Hospital
Hudson, Wisconsin

Hospitals have come a long way since Mr. & Mrs. Stephen C. Phipps helped finance the 1953 opening of Hudson Hospital for Hudson, Wisconsin. Just look at Hudson Health Campus's new, 79,000-square foot replacement hospital and 59,000-square foot clinic, with interior designed by NELSON. The two-story facility, comprising admitting, emergency department, primary and secondary clinics, 30-bed inpatient wing, procedure center, imaging, laboratory, pharmacy, physical therapy, health resource center, cafe, administration, gift shop and expresso bar, incorporates ancient feng shui principles, implemented with C. Suzanne Bates, IIDA, CID, of Design Syndicate Inc., and contemporary design in a healing environment that addresses patients, families and staff alike. The combination is quite potent. Patients and visitors warmly praise the new space, where "main street" public corridors and "interior street" corridors for patients and staff lead to interiors enriched by daylight and views, natural colors, offset lighting, quality materials such as wood, art glass and carpet, and residential-style furnishings. Such unique, feng shui-inspired details as sculpture at the entrance to calm visitors, art niches in corridors that act as "speed bumps," and painted "headboards" on walls to provide visible support ensure that Hudson Hospital will give personalized attention to all who need its care.

**Opposite left:** "Main street" corridor.

**Above:** Winter Garden.

**Right:** Cafe.

**Far right:** Inpatient or extended recovery room.

**Photography:** Philip Prowse.

Bank of America
New York, New York

**Above:** Reception area and connecting stair, 30th floor.

**Left:** Reception area, 33rd floor.

**Opposite right:** Executive board room, 30th floor.

**Photography**: Mark Henninger, Imagic Digital.

Customer service is vital to Bank of America, whose consumer and commercial banking operations serve more than one in four households in the United States, and its importance is dramatically revealed at a handsome, new, 192,000-square foot, eight-level office for Global Corporate and Investment Banking at 40 West 57th Street in midtown Manhattan, designed by NELSON. The facility comprises private offices, open work areas, pantries, copy areas, conference rooms, audio-visual rooms, executive board room, executive floor, reception areas, mail room and network equipment room (NER), accommodating some 600 employees and Bank customers in a classic, mid-Modern corporate environment of curly maple, stone, clear and decorative glass, Venetian plaster and glass tile. Overcoming three on-site problems—turning the building's S-shaped floor plan to advantage by grouping support/communal spaces in the central core and private and open office areas in the wings, clustering open work stations around large existing columns, and treating existing connecting stair and elevator penetrations as design

**Above:** Conference room, 33rd floor.

**Top:** View of conference room from reception area, 33rd floor.

features—the design team has created a seamless blend of technology, strategy and design for the Bank. Comments John Byrne, business support manager and senior vice president/ asset management group for the Bank, "NELSON's vision of what the floors should be from both a form and function standpoint led to a final product that works well and looks sensational."

# Oliver Design Group

The Tower at Erieview
Suite 2900
1301 East Ninth Street
Cleveland, OH 44114
216.696.7300
216.696.5834 (Fax)
www.oliver-design.com

Oliver Design Group

**Oliver Design Group**

Vocational Guidance Services
Cleveland, Ohio

Architecture is making a difference for Vocational Guidance Services, a private, nonprofit organization in Cleveland that has provided vocational training and job placement services to individuals with disabilities or economic disadvantages throughout northeast Ohio since 1890. The organization has seen its capability— and spirits—soar with the completion of its new, 36,200-square foot, two-story Training Center, designed by Oliver Design Group. On a site adjacent to its current inner city location, the new facility welcomes the community with a spacious plaza, accessible front door, and modern, well equipped and environmentally sensitive training facilities for up to 325 students with administrative support space for their instructors. The radiant interior and its 12 training laboratories focus on a "hearth" space, the two-story, daylight-filled Sarah C. Dickenson Commons, where students and faculty can meet, served by the Guidance Grill, a commercial kitchen that is also a food service instructional laboratory, and the state-of-the-art Kacalieff Community Room, which accommodates large group activities. Not surprisingly, Mark Hauserman, VGS board president, praises the Training Center as "a beautiful, functional facility."

**Above left:** Plaza and entrance.

**Above right:** Views (from top down) of Community Room, Classroom and Commons.

**Opposite:** Ramp and stair.

**Photography:** Dan Cunningham.

# Oliver Design Group

## International Consulting Firm
## Cleveland, Ohio

**Left:** Hard Rock Cafe.

**Above right:** Reception.

**Below left:** Consultant's office.

**Below center:** Kitchen adjoining conference center.

**Opposite:** Public area.

**Photography:** Dan Cunningham.

Change is good—except when it's bad. An International Consulting Firm identified its concerns when it retained Oliver Design Group to design its new, 33,500-square foot, two-floor office for 157 employees. As occupants of the Consulting Firm's first office to implement new space standards—reducing assignable work areas 33 to 75 percent—Cleveland personnel were determined to protect the importance of the individual and the quality of the work environment. As a result, conference rooms are the same size as partners' offices or two consultants' offices for easy reconfiguration, corridors are dual-loaded to achieve maximum density, a spacious conference center, inviting food service kitchen and comfortable employee lounge provide much appreciated amenities, and a blend of daylight, halogen lighting and concealed fluorescent lighting keeps the high-density space from feeling isolated or confined. The strength of this pivotal design is expressed in a managing director's comment: "Our staff is ecstatic with our new space and the work Oliver Design Group did for us."

**Oliver Design Group**

Heinen's Fine Foods
Cleveland, Ohio

**Above Left:** Reception.

**Top right:** Meat & seafood area.

**Above right:** Open-plan area.

**Left:** Boardroom.

**Opposite:** Typical store interior.

**Photography:** Dan Cunningham.

In an age of retail mergers and acquisitions, it's no small accomplishment for 18-store Heinen's Fine Foods to declare, "We look forward to continuing to be a family-owned and operated supermarket serving the families of Cleveland." Not long after Joseph Heinen founded Heinen's in 1929, the retailer committed itself to "meet and exceed customer expectations and to treat our employees as family." The commitment clearly extends to Heinen's new corporate office, an attractive, 32,000-square foot, one-story space for 169 employees in a high-bay office complex that has been designed by Oliver Design Group. The office connects with the store interiors, which Oliver Design Group also designs, in terms of color, ceiling and soffit detail. The new environment also takes employees from an outmoded bullpen to a modern setting of open-plan work stations with integrated illumination, power, data distribution and storage, and interior private offices that let everyone share daylight and views. It's not like shopping at Heinen's, but it's nearly as good.

## Oliver Design Group

Day, Ketterer Ltd.
Canton, Ohio

The oldest law firm in Stark County, Ohio, and one of its largest, Day Ketterer Ltd. wanted its new, 26,000-square foot office for 72 employees in downtown Canton to stand out without being lavish or too avant-garde. After all, Day Ketterer was founded in 1872 by William R. Day, Secretary of the Treasury and Supreme Court Justice under President William McKinley. To transform the top two floors within an historic storefront structure into a modern law office, Oliver Design Group placed partner and associate offices along the perimeter, framed by large, glazed walls and side lights to let daylight penetrate the interior, and positioned skylights over the interior stair and adjacent reception area. The library acts as a hub for the contemporary interior. Partner, Robert E. Roland describes the space as fitting Day Ketterer "like a well tailored suit."

**Top left:** Reception.
**Above left:** Cafe.
**Far left:** Library.
**Left:** Boardroom.
**Photography:** Dan Cunningham.

# OWP/P

111 West Washington Street
Suite 2100
Chicago, IL 60602
312.332.9600
312.332.9601 (Fax)
www.owpp.com

Betzold Research & Trading, Inc.
Chicago, Illinois

**Above left:** Entrance and reception.

**Above right:** Proscenium-like transition space.

**Right:** Ceiling panels and LED screen.

**Opposite:** Trading floor.

**Photography:** Steve Hall/Hedrich Blessing.

A recent move from a suburban Chicago office to a new, visually commanding, 12,800-square foot downtown headquarters,designed by OWP/P, marks a bold step forward for Betzold Research & Trading. The fixed-income securities dealer, founded in 1994 by Nicholas W. Betzold, Jr., chairman and CEO, has become a lot more visible to the investment community, thanks to its state-of-the-art trading facility for 90 employees. Supporting Betzold's belief that "trading is performance art," traders sit on a raised platform in the center of a lively, horseshoe-shaped trading floor equipped with suspended LED screens, finely crafted work stations, floating wire mesh ceiling panels, exposed cables and gleaming, patterned metal panel partitions. Not only is the approach from the entrance and circulation spine to the trading floor dramatized by translucent glass panels used as a scrim, the trading floor is positioned so "somebody going to a late train can look up and see something wonderful." Offices, data center and break area with limited food service complete this showcase of high technology that Chicagoans will be looking up to in more ways than one.

## OWP/P

Tandus Showroom
Chicago, Illinois

If one of the carpet industry's major challenges today is creating unified images for companies with multiple brands that preserve each brand's identity, persuasive solution is now on display at the new, 4,000-square foot Tandus Group showroom in Chicago's Merchandise Mart. What distinguishes the design by OWP/P is its flexibility to display products, accommodate educational needs and host special events. Carpet by the three Tandus brands, Crossley, C&A and Monterey, are shown in designated floor locations along an angled path that connects the entire facility. The path, which divides the showroom into an active, open space with a mobile panel system for product displays and storage, and a serene, enclosed space for conference rooms, kitchen, coffee bar and additional storage, takes customers exactly where Tandus wants them.

**Above:** Product displays in showroom.

**Right:** Conference room.

**Opposite:** Entry with view of serene space.

**Photography:** Chris Barrett/Hedrich Blessing.

## Northwest Community Hospital
## Arlington Heights, Illinois

**Left:** The Veranda.
**Above:** Skylight detail.
**Below left:** Servery.
**Right:** Entrance.
**Opposite:** The Rotunda.
**Photography:** Craig Dugan at Hedrich Blessing.

A space with low ceilings, virtually no natural light and a perfect view of the mechanical system was also the perfect location for the new cafeteria. Campus-wide convenience was the driver, so Northwest Community Hospital, a respected, 563-bed hospital in Arlington Heights, Illinois, and its architect, OWP/P, used this space to update an obsolete cafeteria to emulate an upscale dining facility and provide 24/7 service. Instead of creating the new, 28,000-square foot, 350-seat "Oasis" cafeteria and kitchen by renovating the existing space, the hospital relocated it in a vacant OR suite so food service would continue uninterrupted during construction. Better yet, the new setting offers a much broader menu, skylights, an indoor garden, waterfalls, handsome architectural detailing and twice as much seating as before in areas of varying size that can be opened as needed for everyday dining and special events. An 80 percent increase in volume and a high patient satisfaction rating confirm the hospital's healthy appetite for its new cafeteria.

# OWP/P

## JMB Realty Corporation
## Chicago, Illinois

From an initial assignment to develop more efficient floor plans on multi-tenant floors, establish consistency and upgrade such public spaces as elevator cabs, restrooms and a sky lobby at Chicago's 900 North Michigan Avenue, OWP/P was subsequently invited to renovate the 18,000-square foot, on-site headquarters of the building's manager, JMB Realty Corporation, a prominent building owner, developer and manager of properties throughout North America. OWP/P's design for JMB Realty demonstrates the power of design by upgrading the company's private offices, open plan layout in the interior,

conferencing space and formal board room through elegant finishes and sophisticated lighting that complement a spectacular art collection.

**Above:** Lobby.

**Left:** Reception desk.

**Photography:** Steve Hall/Hedrich Blessing

# Perkins Eastman

115 Fifth Avenue
New York, NY 10003
212.353.7200 (Tel)
212.353.7676 (Fax)
www.perkinseastman.com

Charlotte
Chicago
Pittsburgh
San Francisco
Shanghai
Stamford
Toronto

**Perkins Eastman**

CB Richard Ellis
Stamford, Connecticut

Real estate professionals are an optimistic lot, but CB Richard Ellis (CBRE) can persuasively defend its global leadership in real estate services based on over 300 offices staffed by nearly 17,000 employees of partner and affiliate offices in over 50 countries. Even giants like CBRE must deal with a multiplicity of people and procedures, nonetheless, as shown in its handsome, new, 18,000-square foot, Stamford, Connecticut office for 60 employees, designed by Perkins Eastman. The facility combines employees of CBRE and Insignia ESG, a firm CBRE acquired in 2003, juxtaposing two distinctly different organizational cultures. To facilitate interaction and communication among the firms' brokerage teams, Perkins Eastman has located them in one area of the floor plan, pushed support functions to the perimeter, and emphasized the public and client transaction areas. The success of CBRE's private offices, open plan team environment, conference facilities, market research department and reception area is confirmed by frequent praise from some of the most demanding critics in real estate, the brokers themselves.

**Top:** Reception.

**Above left:** Corridor and pantry entry.

**Above right:** Conference room.

**Opposite:** Main corridor.

**Photography:** Woodruff & Brown.

# Perkins Eastman

Fuji Photo Film U.S.A.
Valhalla, New York

The words "print, share, store" project with the clarity of perfectly printed photographs from the 30-foot-long graphic mural at the reception area of Fujifilm's new, 150,000-square foot, three-floor headquarters for sales and marketing in Valhalla, New York. A visitor simply can't miss them. After all, the new mission statement for Fuji Photo Film U.S.A. that provided these words has played a major role in the development of the award-winning facility. In retaining Perkins Eastman to design a new North American home office for 370 employees, Fujifilm, a leading provider of imaging and information solutions, sought to reflect its identity as well as foster collaboration and encourage information sharing among its people. Open space and open-plan work stations dominate the work environment enhanced by conference rooms, breakout areas and main lobby/entry-way, all accessorized with monitors, plasma screens and product displays that tell the Fujifilm story to staff and visitors alike. The relatively few private offices are located in the interior and configured to double as meeting rooms, so the majority of workers may enjoy the daylight and spectacular views of northern Westchester County. Congratulating Perkins Eastman for its achievement, Fujifilm has happily noted, "We continue to receive compliments on the space which is a true reflection of your design professionalism."

**Above left:** Conference room.

**Above right:** Reception.

**Opposite lower left:** Breakout/training.

**Opposite lower right:** Open-plan area.

**Photography:** Jeff Goldberg/Esto, Ben Schneider/Unifor.

# Perkins Eastman

## The Dannon Company
## Greenburgh, New York

**Right:** Waiting area.

**Below right:** Main corridor.

**Bottom right:** Teaming room.

**Opposite:** Reception desk.

**Photography:** Woodruff & Brown.

Every day, the Dannon Company sells and produces six million cups of Dannon® yogurt in almost 100 flavors, styles and sizes. Does that seem like a lot of yogurt? Consider that Dannon®, sold under the names Dannon and Danone, is the world's best-selling brand of yogurt, and Dannon's France-based parent company, The Danone Group, is the worldwide leader in water and fresh dairy products. Such in-gredients have provided the recipe for Dannon's new and distinctly European-accented, 60,900-square foot, two-story U.S. head-quarters in Greenburgh, New York, designed by Perkins Eastman. Given the company's ambitious design brief to move most of the staff from private offices to open-plan work stations (70 percent open-plan to 30 percent private), develop new office design standards, specify European products, integrate the Dannon® brand into the interior design, and rework the color scheme, Perkins Eastman was able to work closely with the CEO and senior management to develop the new facility. The "flavor" of the contemporary environment is complex: open, group-oriented, elegant, forward-thinking, timeless—and unmistakably Dannon's.

**Perkins Eastman**

Tosco
Old Greenwich, Connecticut

Americans may be nostalgic about the 1980s, but that doesn't necessarily endear the architecture of the period to companies doing business within its confines. For oil refiner Tosco, a desire to modernize its 1980s headquarters in Old Greenwich, Connecticut was part of an overall strategy to integrate existing spaces into a new, 22,800-square foot environment for 50 employees, resolve code requirements, create higher ceiling heights despite tight slab-to-slab conditions, and update power and data infrastructure. The new design, by Perkins Eastman, has given Tosco a fresh approach to its boardroom, private offices, open-plan space, executive suite, data center, small lunch room, fitness center and private art collection. Occupying newly revitalized interiors appointed in such materials as sapelle wood, wool carpet, fine fabrics, and leather, Tosco has the best of both worlds, enriching the highlights of the original space with contemporary design concepts and the latest technology.

**Top:** Boardroom.
**Above left:** Reception.
**Left:** Rotunda.
**Photography:** Paul Warchol.

# Perkins+Will

800.837.9455
www.perkinswill.com

Atlanta
Beijing
Boston
Calgary
Charlotte/RTP
Chicago
Dallas
Houston
Los Angeles
Miami
Minneapolis
New York
Seattle
Shanghai
Vancouver

## Perkins+Will

### Time Warner Center
### New York, New York

Extended corporate families must acknowledge their group and individual identities just as extended families do. Time Warner, Inc. one of the worlds largest media companies, recently met the challenge with diplomacy and style at its new Manhattan headquarters, Time Warner Center at Columbus Circle. The 17-floors designed by Perkins+Will in collaboration with Mancini • Duffy provide 1,600 employees with 550,000 square-feet of general offices, executive floors, a 225-seat cafeteria, a screening theater complex, boardroom and pre-function area, and training rooms. To establish continuity and express individuality among Time Warner's businesses the interior design provides universal standards for offices, work stations and conference spaces, a universal location on each floor for support services, and dedicated finishes and conference spaces, to the occupants' identity. The result: a handsome yet nuanced family portrait in wood, stone, terrazzo and modern furnishings.

**Top right:** Cafeteria.
**Above left:** Reception.
**Above right:** Corridor.
**Opposite:** Elevator lobby.
**Photography:** Peter Paige.

# Perkins+Will

## Sonnenshein Nath & Rosenthal LLP
## Chicago, Illinois

Hearing clients say you consistently meet and exceed their expectations is uncommon praise in today's service-oriented economy, so the law firm of Sonnenschein Nath & Rosenthal can rightly claim to be on the cutting edge of legal services. A good example of Sonnenschein's commitment is its new, 16,000-square foot prototype office environment in Chicago, one of nine U.S. locations for its 700 attorneys, that Perkins+Will designed to achieve higher space utilization and greater operational flexibility. Comprising general office spaces, a video conferencing facility and a cafe, the prototype seeks to develop a universal office size for both partners and associates, and to implement a wireless network. The prototype tests several parallel design templates created to explore four key planning issues identified by Sonnenschein personnel, namely community, functionality, adaptability and quality. While testing continues, facility management costs in the new space have already dropped 85 percent.

**Left:** Corridor.
**Right:** Lobby.
**Lower left:** Private office.
**Bottom:** Cafe.

**Photography:** Steve Hall and Craig Dugan/Hedrich Blessing.

## Perkins+Will

### Haworth Center
### Chicago, Illinois

It's a big step to advance from a maker of office furniture to a solutions-driven resource for entire workspaces offering fully integrated architectural systems of furniture, modular walls, raised flooring, ceilings, HVAC, lighting, sound, power, voice and data. Not surprisingly, the new, 29,000-square foot showroom installed in Chicago's Merchandise Mart by Haworth, Inc., one of America's top office furniture manufacturers, departs boldly from standard showroom design. The award-winning facility, designed by Perkins+Will, embodies Haworth's new product platform of "adaptable workspace," "designed performance" and "global perspective" in dramatic settings that combine good design and engineering, holistic thinking about human performance, and green design principles with fully integrated architectural systems. Consequently, the show- room, sales office and conference facility, graced by a large reflecting pool and live plantings, evoke a dramatically better way to work that most visitors would love to take back to their own offices.

**Above left:** Private office setting.

**Top right:** Reflecting pool and brand graphics.

**Mid right:** Open plan work area setting.

**Lower right:** Café and floor product display.

**Opposite:** Corridor and entry plantings.

**Photography:** Steve Hall and Craig Dugan/Hedrich Blessing.

**Perkins+Will**

Winthrop & Weinstine
Minneapolis, Minnesota

How can a business conduct the consolidation of existing offices as a positive change? For Winthrop & Weinstine, a law firm founded in 1979 where 75 attorneys lead a work force of 280, the recent merging of its Minneapolis and St. Paul offices in a new, 72,000-square foot, four-story Minneapolis office wisely balances operational efficiency with superior environment. The design by Perkins+Will simultaneously increases space utilization and flattens internal hierarchy by reducing six standard office sizes to three. Interface communication and circulation has been enhanced by inserting a four-story interconnecting stairway. The design improves morale and attracts new staff by offering handsome and comfortable accommodations for personalized and collaborative work. A hallmark of the new office is its large gallery. Here, staff can gather for meals, meetings and social events, exploring possibilities beyond the scope of more conventional private offices, open work areas, meeting rooms and support space.

**Upper left:** Reception.

**Upper right:** Interior staircase.

**Above:** Conference room.

**Photography:** Christopher Barrett/Hedrich Blessing.

# Roger Ferris + Partners LLC

90 Post Road East
Westport, CT 06880
203.222.4848
203.222.4856 (Fax)
www.ferrisarch.com

## Roger Ferris + Partners LLC

**Roger Ferris + Partners LLC**

Sempra Metals & Concentrates Corp.
Stamford, Connecticut

A heated global economy is changing the fortunes of nations overnight, and the resulting demand for metals keeps such companies as Sempra Metals & Concentrates Corp. extremely busy. A recent renovation of an existing, 40,000-square foot, one-story office in Stamford, Connecticut, designed by Roger Ferris + Partners, testifies to the intensity of metals trading in today's commodities markets. In the facility's trading floor, private offices, conference room, data center and pantry, Sempra Metals has the means for 24/7 trading operations by some 150 employees, client-specific communication and interaction, and abundant natural lighting with total privacy and no direct sunlight or glare. The new workplace, enclosed by an elegant, minimal curtain wall of metal panels and translucent glass channel glazing, gives Sempra Metals an effective and handsome business tool for serving the world's major mining, smelting and refining companies, as well as leading base metal fabricators and consumers.

**Above left:** Conference room.

**Top right:** Exterior wall detail.

**Above:** View of trading.

**Left:** Trading floor.

**Opposite:** Chinese glass facade.

**Photography:** Paul Rivera/ Arch Photo.

**Roger Ferris + Partners LLC**

FactSet Research Systems, Inc.
Norwalk, Connecticut

If you supply financial intelligence to the international investment community, offering over 200 databases drawn from stock markets, research firms, and other major sources, as well as clients' own proprietary data, you must be efficient, accurate and reliable. How well FactSet Research Systems understands this can be seen in its new, 200,000-square foot, five-story headquarters in Norwalk, Connecticut, designed by Roger Ferris + Partners. Not only does the facility, encompassing reception, private and open offices, A/V-equipped conference rooms, boardroom, data center, kitchen and cafeteria, have 24/7/365 power capability—backed by an on-site generator, UPS and disaster control support rooms. FactSet's headquarters also maintains optimum conditions for staff and visitors. While each department is placed around the core infrastructure that directly supports it, a dignified environment of beech millwork, stainless steel, glass and limestone in reception and boardroom eloquently declares, "Welcome to FactSet."

**Top:** Reception area.

**Above right:** Corner conference room.

**Left:** Board room.

**Opposite:** Reception seating.

**Photography:** Paul Rivera/ Arch Photo.

**Roger Ferris + Partners LLC**　　PanAmSat
Wilton, Connecticut

Buck Rogers, Captain Kirk and Luke Skywalker are nowhere in sight at PanAmSat's handsome new, 75,000-square foot headquarters in Wilton, Connecticut, designed by Roger Ferris + Partners. Then again, being the satellite-based communications pioneer that launched the world's first privately owned international satellite in 1984, as well as an industry powerhouse fielding 22 satellites with over 900 usable transponders, 700-plus employees, seven technical ground facilities and 13 offices on five continents, PanAmSat is serious about its role as a leading distributor of entertainment and information. As a result, its executive offices, program support rooms, boardroom and teleconference rooms constitute a contemporary workplace of maple wood, carpet and glass that is sophisticated yet understated, where 254 employees serve a network reaching 98 percent of the world's population.

**Above left :** Video tele-confrence room.

**Above right:** Reception area.

**Far left:** Board room.

**Photography:** Woodruff & Brown Photography.

# Roger Ferris + Partners LLC

**Above left:** Conference/break room.

**Above right:** Reception seating.

**Bottom right:** Entry portal.

**Photography:** Woodruff & Brown Photography.

# Sasaki Associates, Inc.

64 Pleasant Street
Watertown, MA 02472
617.926.3300
617.924.2748 (Fax)
www.sasaki.com

Sasaki Associates, Inc.

# Sasaki Associates, Inc.

## Nutter McClennen & Fish LLP
## Boston, Massachusetts

Founded by U.S. Supreme Court Justice Louis D. Brandeis and Samuel D. Warren in 1879, Nutter McClennen & Fish recently occupied a new, 135,000-square foot, 450-person office in Boston's Seaport District, designed by Sasaki Associates, that is more stylish and efficient than might be expected from one of New England's oldest and most distinguished law firms. However, Nutter attributes the success of its 160 lawyers to such timeless values as professional excellence, ingenuity and foresight in serving clients. Accordingly, the four-story design places the conference center on the two middle floors with the reception area on the lower of the two, provides such additional spaces as standard, 140-square foot private offices for attorneys, law library and fitness center, and appoints interiors in millwork paneling, stone flooring, contemporary furnishings and a stainless-steel-and-glass staircase cantilevered around a wood pylon that anchors the conference center. Its provisions to serve clients is exemplified by the conference center, where paneled doors pivot to extend the conference space into the reception room for private functions, and folding doors dividing individual conference rooms open to create a 2,000-square foot meeting and social area--whatever serves clients best.

**Above left:** Elevator lobby.

**Above right:** "The Bistro," informal meeting and dining area.

**Right:** Secretarial work stations.

**Far right:** Conference center.

**Opposite:** Reception area and staircase.

**Photography:** Richard Mandelkorn.

# Sasaki Associates, Inc.

Cetrulo & Capone LLP
Boston, Massachusetts

Daylight and discretion mark the new, 33,000-square foot, 120-person Boston office of Cetrulo & Capone, a law firm founded in 1995 that also maintains offices in New York and Providence, Rhode Island. The qualities of this handsome facility, designed by Sasaki Associates, complement the practice, which provides legal services in litigation and business matters to clients in all six New England states, and New York. Occupying a single floor in the East Office Building at the Seaport World Trade Center, the space offers a custom, built-in bench along a window wall with sweeping views of Boston's waterfront and Logan International Airport, yet admits daylight and obscured views into the large, interior conference room to preserve privacy. Similar attention to such details as the floating ceiling planes that define entry and seating areas, and the color coordination of administrative work stations with interior walls, provides the finishing touches.

**Above:** Window wall seating for scenic views.

**Right:** Large conference room.

**Far right:** Reception area.

**Photography:** Lucy Chen.

# Sasaki Associates, Inc.

## Biogen Idec
## Cambridge, Massachusetts

Eight weeks to develop a new board room and adjacent servery in Cambridge, Massachusetts for Biogen Idec, the world's third-largest biotechnology company, may stand out as a fast-track project in the design world, but the pace is not unusual for Biogen Idec. After all, the company that commissioned the finely detailed, 1400-square foot suite, designed by Sasaki Associates to employ state-of-the-art technology, was formed in November 2003 through the merger of Biogen and IDEC Pharmaceuticals, two dynamic young companies that have won respect for the development, manufacture and commercialization of innovative health care products. Incorporating an audio-visual system with teleconferencing and video presentations, media such as DVD, laptop hook-up and cable TV, and lighting with three level settings, it is controlled by a simple, touch-activated panel to enhance business life, much as Biogen Idec's products enhance life for patients.

**Sasaki Associates, Inc.**

The TJX Family Memorial Garden
Framingham, Massachusetts

The TJX Companies, Inc., which operates T.J. Maxx, Marshalls, HomeGoods, A.J. Wright and Bob's Stores in the United States, Winners and HomeSense in Canada, and T.K. Maxx in Europe, commissioned Sasaki Associates to design a 2,000-square foot memorial garden at its Framingham, Massachusetts headquarters for seven associates who died on September 11, 2001. The garden lies adjacent to the southwest entry to the headquarters because the entry directly faces the parking structure and receives heavy use by associates, and offers the sunniest and quietest area on site. Families, friends and associates of the seven women who enter it find a contemplative place of birch trees, teak benches, trellises, bluestone pavers, a curved glass sculpture framing seven panels that identify each woman, and plantings that feature evergreens along with roses, lilacs and hydrangea, which were favorites of the women. TJX will ensure that the garden stays fresh and colorful.

**Above:** Overhead view of the garden.

**Right:** A close-up of the panels identifying the lost associates.

**Photography:** Richard Mandelkorn.

240

# Silvester + Tafuro, Inc.

50 Washington Street
South Norwalk, CT 06854
203.866.9221
203.838.2436 (Fax)

Silvester + Tafuro, International
Unit 7, 2nd Floor
Culvert House
Culvert Road
Battersea, London SW11 SAP
United Kingdom
44.207.498.5534
44.207.498.5574 (Fax)

www.silvestertafuro.com

# Silvester + Tafuro, Inc.

## American Airlines Admirals Club
Newark, New Jersey

Though it represented the third phase of American Airlines' extensive renovation of its terminal, connector and satellite facilities at Newark International Airport, Newark, New Jersey, the handsome new, 6,700-square foot, 140-seat Admirals Club, designed by Silvester + Tafuro, arrived not a moment too soon. Security procedures introduced at Newark and other U.S. airports since September 11, 2001 have encouraged travelers to arrive earlier and stay longer. Not surprisingly, business people flying American Airlines have found its 45 Admirals Clubs to be a welcome refuge from crowds as well as a better way to spend "dwell time."

To create a warm, comfortable atmosphere, develop a sense of flow from room to room, and diminish the "railroad car" feeling of the 53-foot by 126-foot space at Newark International, the designers set rooms at 45-degree angles, embraced non-linear forms, highlighted a circular canted wall and ran a skylight along the full length of the club. What do business travelers think of the new Admirals Club? Try finding an empty seat in the three full-service conference rooms, nine individual work stations, reception area, bar area and window-side seating lounge.

**Above:** View from reception area.

**Opposite, lower left:** Window-side seating lounge.

**Photography:** Peter Paige.

# Silvester + Tafuro, Inc.

## D-Parture Spa
### Newark, New Jersey

Charles Lindbergh and Amelia Earhart would have found it all quite amusing. Today's travelers are finding time, money and opportunity in the newest airports to eat, shop and conduct business between flights. How about a haircut and shampoo, massage, manicure or pedicure in a stylish, upscale and calming environment just steps from your gate? It's the latest option, thanks to D-Parture Spa at Terminal C of Newark International Airport, Newark, New Jersey, designed by Silvester+Tafuro Design. Once your attention is captured by the jaunty mahogany, mosaic tile and slate storefront, you enter the compact, 525-square foot store to discover a studio-like setting that surrounds you in an oasis of blond birch wood cabinetry, blond hardwood flooring, suspended glass shelving and Italian glass pendant lighting. Ah... what flight, you say?

**Below left:** Retail setting for personal care and cosmetics, make-up and shampoo for sale.

**Opposite:** Storefront.

**Photography:** Peter Paige.

## Silvester + Tafuro, International

### Holideck
London, United Kingdom

**Left:** Entry.
**Below:** Lounge.
**Photography:** Keith Perry.

You can meet such interesting people wandering through airports. In fact, research by KLM Ground Services reveals that virtually every category of airline passenger—leisure, family and group travelers as well as business travelers—seeks better airport accommodations. Rather than develop another business-oriented airline club, KLM Ground Services recently enlisted Silvester+Tafuro's London office to transform its futuristic vision of an airport lounge into "Holideck" at Terminal 4 of London's Heathrow International Airport. This gracious, 8,052-square foot space takes the unprecedented step of providing first-class entertainment facilities for both business and leisure class passengers on three levels or "decks," regardless of their tickets or airlines. Besides offering standard business amenities, Holideck proffers such delights as a child-friendly Family Lounge, an Interactive Zone for digital diversions, and the "Haven," where passengers can sink into sleeper chairs to travel wherever their dreams take them.

# Silvester + Tafuro, Inc.

## Hudson News - Euro Cafe
Chicago, Illinois

Cappuccino with your magazines? Now with periodicals and cafe fare seemingly inseparable, Chicago's Midway Regional Airport cherishes its new Hudson News-Euro Cafe, a co-branded, upscale, 2,568-square foot store, designed by Silvester+Tafuro. Here, a newsstand selling magazines and newspapers from around the world joins a European-style cafe selling pastry, fruit juices and freshly roasted coffee in a delectable blend of cherry wood cabinetry, granite flooring and counter tops and a soffit depicting Chicago's skyline.

**Above:** Selling floor.
**Right:** Storefront.
**Photography:** Peter Paige.

# Silvester + Tafuro, International

## Sabre
## Corporate Offices
London, United Kingdom

Sabre, the leading provider of technology that enables the travel industry and enhances airline/supplier operations, with 2001 revenues of $2.1 billion, has grown so steadily in London that the original, 2,500-square foot fit-out is now a new, 55,000-square foot, three-story office, designed by Silvester + Tafuro's London office. Having worked with Sabre for five years, the design firm presided over the continual expansion of the initial space. However, the new office stems from a thorough review of existing space, a new master plan, and a fresh take on open planning and work station design that should keep Sabre on top of the travel world.

**Above:** Customer service office space.

**Below left:** Conference room.

**Below right:** Building entrance.

**Photography:** Vaughn E. Ryall.

# Susman Tisdale Gayle

4330 South Mopac Expwy.
Suite 100
Austin, TX 78735
512.899.3500
512.899.3501 (Fax)
www.stgarchitects.com

**Susman Tisdale Gayle**

Winstead Sechrest & Minick, PC
Austin, Texas

**Top left:** Conference room.

**Above left:** Library.

**Above right:** Reception seen from core area.

**Opposite below right:** Open work stations.

**Photography:** Paul Bardagjy.

Austin, Texas, capital of the Lone Star State, gateway the to Texas Hill Country and Highland Lakes, and home of the University of Texas, appreciates being "impressive but not extravagant." This understated attitude characterizes the new, 50,000-square foot, two-story office for Winstead Sechrest & Minick, PC, a law firm founded some 30 years ago that employs more than 300 attorneys in eight locations. For 70 attorneys and 45 supporting employees in Austin, Susman Tisdale Gayle arranged the private offices, multi-purpose room, video conference room, business center with visitor office, catering kitchen and serving gallery, satellite libraries and break room into radiating floor plans where conference facilities counteract off-center elevator lobbies. While entirely pragmatic, the office offers daylight, even at the ends of hallways, dramatic panaramic views, especially through the main conference room, and local ambiance, created with color choices and artwork, to employees and visitors alike.

**Susman Tisdale Gayle**

Clark, Thomas & Winters, PC
Austin, Texas

**Above left:** Reception seating.

**Top Right:** Elevator lobby.

**Above:** Secretarial stations.

**Opposite:** Reception.

**Photography:** Paul Bardagjy.

Founded as Looney and Clark in 1938, the Austin-based law firm of Clark, Thomas & Winters, PC has deep roots in the Lone Star State that were established when its founders, Everett Looney and Edward Clark, served Texas Attorney General and future Governor James V. Allred as assistants. The firm's heritage, quality and reliability are reflected in the fact that it has only occupied three offices in its history. Thus, its recent move to a new, 91,000 square foot, three-floor space, designed by Susman Tisdale Gayle in collaboration with Gensler, provided an excellent opportunity to create a modern, efficient and attractive workplace for 142 attorneys and 140 supporting employees. While wasting nothing in laying out the private offices, conference center, training facility and lunch-room, the design emphasizes visual interest as well as circulation flow, insetting secretarial stations to widen corridors, finishing surfaces in limestone, anigre and cherry veneers, and Venetian plaster, and showcasing the firm's Texas history and memorabilia in custom-made, inter-changeable and secure display fixtures. There's even an illuminated star above the main reception area that needs no explanation.

**Susman Tisdale Gayle**

Broadjump
Austin, Texas

Considering the floor's sheer size, the problem facing a new, 90,000 square foot, single-level headquarters in Austin, Texas, for Broadjump, a provider of broadband software for DSL, cable, and wireless broadband providers, was inescapable. How could 350 employees be spared a "sea of cubes"? The new facility, designed by Susman Tisdale Gayle, is an open office punctuated by private offices, software testing laboratories and customer area--the product of an aggressive schedule, tight budget, complex lighting requirements and sustainability issues. Accordingly, private offices subdivide open areas, exposed ceilings add height, interior walls stop short of the ceiling, three colorways of carpet minimize waste and introduce patterns, indirect lighting and skylights reduce ceiling reflections, and low-VOC materials and a two-week pause between construction and move-in stet minimized off-gassing. Not bad for a 16-week project!

**Above left:** Entry lobby.
**Bottom right:** Reception.
**Bottom left:** Corridor.
**Photography:** Mark Knight.

# Ted Moudis Associates

305 East 46th Street
New York, NY 10017
212.308.4000
212.644.8673 (Fax)
www.tedmoudis.com

One Financial Place
440 South LaSalle Street
Chicago, IL 60605
312.663.0130 (Fax)
312.663.0138

# Ted Moudis Associates

Deloitte Global Headquarters
New York, New York

The design concept for the Deloitte Global Headquarters and conferencing suite was inspired by the firm's interest to support its people and work processes, while reflecting their progressive image through technology and global influences. A lot of time was invested in best practice research, to benchmark each function within the space and how to best design for that need. For a visiting executive needing to check their luggage, work within a private, satellite office, and converse with colleagues or host different types of meetings and events, these functions became important elements of the space. Flexibility was also important, requiring that the boardroom, designed to seat 42, could also be split into two smaller rooms. The servery adjacent to the boardroom has the capability to accomodate multiple meetings at one time, or be divided to service dedicated rooms.

**Above:** Elevator lobby.
**Near left:** Traders servery.
**Left:** Boardroom.
**Far left:** Waiting area.
**Lower left:** Trading floor.
**Photography:** Peter Paige.

ICAP North America, Inc. the world's largest interdealer broker with an average daily transaction volume in excess of $700 billion, has moved to a new, 120,000-square foot, two-level office for 800 employees in Jersey City, New Jersey, designed by Ted Moudis Associates. Interestingly, much of the facility revolves around an expansive, 575-position trading floor meant to appear organized and flexible—despite the standard trading room's reputation as a chaotic place. To manage the trading environment, the design couples a high-ceiling solution incorporating cutting-edge lighting and acoustical equipment with furniture that readily adapts to new technology. Additionally, two serveries where included in the design to offer a temporary get-away for the busy traders. Of course, the facility's reception area, executive boardroom and executive offices receive their due as well. Their classic furnishings and modern aesthetics combine timeless elegance with advanced technology that, in stark contrast to the trading floor, remains discreetly inconspicuous.

# Ted Moudis Associates

## Satellite Asset Management, L.P.
## New York, New York

Rapid growth can make an organization's facility more challenging to design, but it's a problem the business world prefers to the opposite scenario. Case in point is the newly renovated and expanded, 26,000-square foot, two-level office in midtown Manhattan for Satellite Asset Management, L.P., a hedge fund with over $5.4 billion dollars in assets under management. When Ted Moudis Associates began designing the renovation of Satellite's existing space on an office tower's 21st floor, there were 10 employees and uncertain anticipated growth. The completed facility, which incorporates the building's 20th and 21st floors, provides 60 employees with private offices, open-plan work stations, executive waiting areas, boardrooms, conference rooms, support space, pantries, custom-designed interconnecting stair— and spectacular views of Rockefeller Center and St. Patrick's Cathedral. Key to the design has been a flexible layout for future growth and development, complemented by a design aesthetic based on a glass-and-stainless-steel frontal system that maximizes daylight and staff interaction, and satisfies the firm's seven partners. In addition, Satellite wanted a facility whose image would be immediately recognized in the financial sector as one of stability and stature, and that's exactly what it has.

**Above:** Reception area with boardroom beyond.

**Right:** Open plan area with perimeter offices.

**Opposite top:** Boardroom.

**Opposite center:** Elevator lobby.

**Photography:** Paul Warchol.

## Ted Moudis Associates

### Zurich Capital Markets
### New York, New York

How do you establish a high level of interest, comfort and efficiency in a 15,000-square foot, one-level New York office for 120 employees built around the activities of a 100-position trading area? For Zurich Capital Markets, a member of Zurich Financial Services and a leading provider of tailored solutions for clients seeking to enhance investment returns, improve asset liquidity, and/or increase the efficiency of portfolio administration, Ted Moudis Associates has created a design featuring innovative, hexagonal trading desk modules, advanced lighting and ventilation technology for low ceilings, and a warm, inviting and appropriately aggressive environment. In the trading area, private offices, conference rooms, elevator lobby and employee lounge, a stylish, contemporary design using pearwood, marble, granite, stainless steel and soft, blue accent lighting keeps traders on their toes.

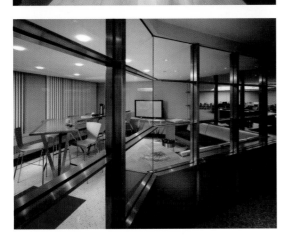

**Top:** Reception area and conference room.

**Above left:** Elevator lobby.

**Above right:** Trading area.

**Left:** Employee lounge.

**Photography:** Peter Paige.

# VOA Associates

234 South Michigan Avenue
Suite 1400
Chicago, Illinois 60604
312.554.1400
312.554.1412 (Fax)
www.voa.com

**VOA Associates**

# VOA Associates

## Adams Street Partners, LLC
## Chicago, Illinois

You learn to respect the past and anticipate the future at Adams Street Partners, one of the world's largest global managers of private equity partnership investments with one of the longest histories. After all, Adams Street and its predecessor organizations have been investing in private equity fund partnerships since 1979 and managing direct investments in private equity since 1972. The firm's new, 40,500-square foot, 1-1/3 floor, 68-person Chicago office, designed by VOA Associates, reflects this nuanced view by incorporating traditional elements with contemporary openness and lightness. Yet the financial industry's tradition of private offices prevails in a handsome environment that surrounds them with support space, conference room/ anteroom, lunchroom, library and reception area. Architectural elements evoking Perisan and Prairie styles that captivated turn-of-the-century Chicago help establish a clear spatial hierarchy that inspires employees and visitors in ways that transcend time.

**Top:** Telephone station.

**Above left:** Reception.

**Above right:** Anteroom outside conference.

**Opposite:** Corridor.

**Photography:** Nick Merrick/Hedrich Blessing.

**VOA Associates**

ABN AMRO/LaSalle Bank
ABN AMRO Plaza- Conference & Training Center
Chicago, Illinois

ABN AMRO Bank intends to be one of the top banks in its peer group. Already a leading, Amsterdam-based international bank with assets of EUR 632.8 billion (June 2004), ABN AMRO employs some 107,000 employees in banking, fund management and leasing at over 3,400 branch offices in more than 60 countries. Keeping employees in top form is essential to the bank's strategy, and the new, 50,000-square foot, two-level Conference and Training Center, designed by VOA Associates, at ABN AMRO Plaza in Chicago enables it to do just that. Conference and training facilities on the 23rd and 24th floors respectively give the 5,000 employees of LaSalle Bank, ABN

AMRO's major U.S. subsidiary, at this location a versatile, interactive environment highlighted by such features as conference rooms equipped with advanced multi-media equipment, circulation and break out areas along the window walls created by offsetting conference rooms from the perimeter, movable walls, mobile furnishings, and a dramatic internal staircase that is the focal point of the main reception area—a potent source of inspiration for current and future leaders of ABN AMRO.

**VOA Associates**　　ABN AMRO Plaza-Cafeteria
Chicago, Illinois

Sometimes the last thing a company wants for a corporate cafeteria is a typical corporate cafeteria. An uplifting example of how to break the mold is the 40,000-square foot, 835-seat cafeteria serving 5,000 employees of LaSalle Bank, the major U.S. subsidiary of Amsterdam-based ABN AMRO Bank, at Chicago's 1.3-million-square-foot ABN AMRO Plaza. The kitchen, servery and two separate dining areas, designed by VOA Associates, manages to combine efficiency, durability, comfort and aesthetics at the same time.

The ingredients of the award-winning design include flexible seating options from booths for two to tables for large groups, architectural elements inspired by art, music and dance that subdivide seating areas, and servery for bakery/cafe, pizza oven, salad bar, deli counter, and hot and cold stations for Mexican, Asian, grilled food and rotisserie. It's not your average corporate cafeteria, for sure.

**Left:** Decorative screen.
**Below left:** Servery.
**Below right:** Dining room.
**Photography:** Chris Barrett/Hedrich Blessing.

# VOA Associates

## ABN AMRO/LaSalle Bank
## ABN AMRO Plaza-General Office Floors
## Chicago, Illinois

Consolidating employees from several locations to ABN AMRO Plaza in downtown Chicago, LaSalle Bank, the major U.S. subsidiary of Amsterdam-based ABN AMRO Bank, achieves what many businesses overlook: creative, best-practice office planning strategies that directly serve core business strategies. The bank's new, 680,000-square foot, 21-floor general office areas for 5,000 employees were designed by VOA Associates to reduce occupancy costs and operational risk, provide flexibility and adaptability to change, improve work flow and adjacencies, and attract and retain an elite work force. In a break from convention, the new general offices feature inboard private offices and 120-degree, open plan work stations exposed to window walls, daylight and outdoor views, smaller individual work stations offset by new huddle rooms, pantries, interactive zones and multiple teaming spaces, and a 10-foot module to facilitate reconfiguration. Clearly, this workplace can keep pace with its work.

**VOA Associates**

ABN AMRO Plaza-Retail Bank
Chicago, Illinois

How do you place a 5,000-square-foot retail branch bank in the lobby of a new, 1.3-million-square-foot high-rise office building in downtown Chicago? Very carefully, to say the least. For LaSalle Bank, the major U.S. subsidiary of Amsterdam-based ABN AMRO Bank, the right response at ABN AMRO Plaza is a bold, contemporary design by VOA Associates that respects the modern image of the office building even as it adds fascinating details of its own. The award-winning retail branch exploits the dynamic image of glowing numbers representing financial statistics to catch the attention of pedestrians in the lobby space and draw them inside a facility with tellers on one side, personal bankers on the other, and an interactive reception area and managers' offices in the center. Before they know it, they may be banking with LaSalle.

**Above left:** Overall frontal view.

**Above right:** Interactive screens.

**Left:** Personal bankers.

**Photography:** Steve Hall/Hedrich Blessing.

# Wolcott Architecture • Interiors

3859 Cardiff Avenue
Culver City, CA 90232
310.204.2290
310.838.6109 (Fax)
www.wolcottai.com

Wolcott Architecture • Interiors

## Wolcott Architecture • Interiors

Houlihan Lokey Howard & Zukin
Los Angeles, California

Having served thousands of clients over 25 years, Los Angeles-based investment banker Houlihan Lokey Howard & Zukin is well established in middle-market corporate finance. The firm is a major player in raising private and public equity for small-cap public and mid-sized private companies, and figures prominently in restructurings and mergers and acquisitions as well. Evidence of its success includes a consistent ranking as one of America's top 20 M&A advisors for the past decade, and the leading position among U.S. investment banks for transactions under $200 million in 2003. Another measure is the recent remodeling of its reception area and boardroom, designed by Wolcott Architecture • Interiors. The handsome, contemporary spaces introduce reception seating, improve security at the entrance and exit—and double boardroom capacity.

**Above:** Boardroom.

**Right and far right:** Reception area.

**Photography:** Marshal Safron.

"Where is the entrance?" A frequent challenge for visitors to contemporary buildings is finding their way inside. When the developer of Watt Plaza, a pair of 25-story Los Angeles office towers built in 1989, asked Wolcott Architecture • Interiors to remodel the existing free-standing entry pavilion and public spaces joining the two structures, the design team committed itself to creating a genuine sense of place and navigable circulation plan. The renovated pavilion,enlivened with a sculpture/ fountain, new security checkpoints, and a fresh image combining granite, glass, perforated steel, maple wood veneer and gypsum, establishes a strong hierarchy of space and a logical spatial progression to direct visitors quickly and easily to their destinations at Watt Plaza. Assessing the 22,000-square foot project, a B.O.M.A. "TOBY" award winner, the developer says, "The end product exceeded all of our expectations."

**Above:** Exterior of entry pavilion.

**Right:** Corridor to elevators.

**Opposite above:** Sculpture/ fountain.

**Opposite below:** View from concierge desk.

**Photography:** Marshal Safron.

**Wolcott Architecture • Interiors**

Caruso Affiliated Holdings
Los Angeles, California

**Above:** Boardroom.

**Left and far left:** Executive office.

**Opposite:** Grand staircase.

**Photography:** Marshal Safron. Mario Carrieri.

Americans' passion for shopping malls is reputed to be cooling off, but that doesn't explain why they still crowd into the unique neighborhood and regional retail centers developed by Caruso Affiliated, a respected Los Angeles-based real estate firm. Under its president and CEO Rick J. Caruso, the company goes to considerable lengths to customize each center it builds, creating a memorable "town center" that respects the character of the surrounding community and the spirit of the residents. What makes this enlightened approach stand out is its ability to generate profits as well as good will. Many of regional and national tenants in Caruso Affiliated properties report some of the highest grossing sales for their chains, securing their loyalty and enabling the firm to start construction of new projects with a minimum of

278

# Wolcott Architecture • Interiors

90 percent pre-leased space. Caruso Affiliated's faith in its own work is exemplified by a new, 25,000-square foot corporate headquarters located at The Grove, a Caruso Affiliated retail center in Los Angeles adjacent to the city's beloved Farmers Market. Wolcott Architecture • Interiors, in association with Diane Johnson Interior Design, gave Mr. Caruso an office with a bird's eye view of The Grove. The design team created a handsome, traditional suite of private offices, open-plan areas and conference rooms, along with the main entry and grand staircase for the building that houses it. Elegant and efficient in character, the facility lets the staff enjoy a residential ambiance at the same time it directs one of the most savvy retail real estate operations in the nation.

**Top:** Reception.
**Above left:** Lounge.
**Above right:** Corridor.

THE PUMA COLLECTION          designed by William Sklaroff

## Subtlety is always in style.

Looking at this ad, you might not have noticed the ceiling. That's the whole point.
Techstyle® Acoustical Ceilings create a clean, monolithic look that emphasizes the
beauty of an entire space.

For literature and our email newsletter,
call toll-free 866-556-1235
or visit www.hunterdouglascontract.com

*Installation:* Lida Baday Showroom, New York, NY
Architect: Zuliani + Associates
4′ x 4′ panels

©2005 Hunter Douglas Inc. ® Trademark of Hunter Douglas Inc.

**HunterDouglasContract**

CEILINGS

# Who Kidnapped Casual Friday?

By Roger Yee

## How the global drive to work faster, cheaper and better is affecting office design in America.

Who would have predicted that Europe's Airbus Industrie would come nowhere in 1970 to overtake Boeing, an American corporate icon, as the world's top passenger airplane builder in 2003, and add insult to injury by rolling out the world's largest passenger aircraft, the 555-seat Airbus A380, in 2005? It's a dramatic reminder that America's economic dominance in the 20th century, hailed as "The American Century" by Henry Luce, the visionary publisher of Time, Fortune and Life magazines, is not guaranteed today. If the United States intends to lead a world where developing nations like Russia, India and China are poised to compete in high technology, it will need to give its people the resources they need to work more effectively. One of the key resources for the work force will surely be the office.

The office? Seen at a glance, even the newest office sustains the image of business as usual. Some people can be seen working in enclosed or "private" offices surrounded by floor-to-ceiling walls and doors, or in completely open or "bullpen" spaces. Far more workers occupy partly open or "open-plan" spaces, defined by partial-height partitions and outfitted with work surfaces, storage units and seating—the "cubicle farm" housing cartoonist Scott Adams' hapless Dilbert—that have become the office standard since the mid-1970s. Still others sit around tables in enclosed conference rooms or open lounges. Has nothing changed?

That depends on whom you ask. American businesses have significantly empowered employees and operations with information technology to remain competitive. While clerical functions have been significantly streamlined, strategic functions have been equipped to generate value through research, creativity and innovation. However, getting into shape for global competition doesn't necessarily require rebuilding the office environment from scratch.

*It's not about the cell phone or PDA*

What's the key determinant of office design? Office work, of course. Despite dot-com era predictions that the modern office population would concentrate on critical thinking, dividing into interdependent components based on teamwork and the technology-enabled ability to work outside the office—collectively called "alternative workplace strategies" or AWS—architects and interior designers report that many organizations continue to maintain conventional clerical and strategic operations under the same roof. In fact, a recent study sponsored by the International Facility Management Association and LaSalle Partners Incorporated indicates that employee participation rates in AWS remain relatively low: 17 percent for team environments and 3 percent for telecommuting.

For Nila Leiserowitz, AIA, a principal and design director of Gensler, the nation's largest interior design firm and an American Institute of Architects Firm of the Year, one of the more satisfying consequences of global competition is that clients are more willing to examine the role of offices in improving business. "Just five years ago," Leiserowitz recalls, "clients still wanted to begin by counting people, desks and files, and reviewing aesthetic choices. Now they want us to explore what their people actually do with space, demonstrate how office design can promote change management, and measure the impact of design on performance. It's a great time to be a designer."

What happens when the need for change becomes compelling? "People see that the basic office components are still in place, but they have new relationships," explains Jack Tanis, director of applied research for Steelcase, the largest office furniture maker in the world. Using such tools of social science as ergonomics, cognitive psychology, social psychology and cultural anthropology, Tanis and his colleagues work with organizations to understand not only how they currently work, but how they want to work and what design can do to better working conditions. He reports that a lot of organizations are discovering that where a group interacts is more important than where individuals work autonomously.

However, a new reliance on teamwork doesn't lessen the need to house individuals in the office. "If the balance between the individual and the group in the office is shifting in favor of the group," notes Ginny B. Baxter, IIDA, ASID, ISFE, senior manager, workplace dynamics, for Herman Miller, a widely admired manufacturer of office furniture, "organizations must still maintain the integrity of the individual." Baxter points out that no U.S. company has moved its operations completely overseas or outside its own premises, and many offices are very productive. "Place still counts," she cautions, "even with information technology keeping everyone connected. We can now do all our shopping on-line, yet we still want neighborhood stores."

*Guess who still has the biggest office*

Just as shoppers expect neighborhood stores to have modern bar-code scanners, in-store promotions and credit card terminals, architects, interior designers and the office furnishings industry agree that the most traditional looking 21st-century offices often require design schemes capable of responding quickly, easily and inexpensively to change. An international economy committed to working faster, cheaper and better, spares nobody.

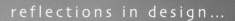

reflections in design...

AERO Bench Series

designed by Liévore/Altherr/Molina
licensed from Sellex

...design *is* a choice

DAVIS

Davis Furniture Ind. Inc.
*Tel* 336 889 2009
*Fax* 336 889 0031
www.davisfurniture.com

*Here is a brief look at the consequences for office design:*

- Private offices: Senior managers, lawyers, human resources directors and selected other middle managers and professionals still enjoy walls and doors that provide privacy and define their rank. Surprise? For all the 1990s fervor about "flattening the pyramid," today's businesses and institutions are hardly more egalitarian. "The private office continues to be needed as a status symbol and refuge for confidentiality," states Lisa Pool, interior design discipline leader for Perkins & Will, a respected architecture firm with offices across the country. "They may be fewer, smaller and less varied," she asserts, "but they rarely surrender their positions along the perimeter."

- Open-plan areas: While floor area allotments for individual work stations in open-plan areas now reflect minimal sizes, partitions between work stations are lower so occupants can see one another and receive more light, alleviating the confinement that dogs the typical "Dilbertville." Equally encouraging, low-cost, versatile and attractive office accessories help individuals customize work stations for specific tasks. "The design of open-plan areas has become fairly standardized," observes Jeff Reuschel, manager of ideation for Haworth, a major U.S. office furniture maker with distinguished European affiliates. "While there's a lot of boiler plate in general offices, it's good boiler plate."

*If alternative workplaces represented the future in the 1990s, why do so few employees occupy them today?*

- Meeting areas: The countless informal gathering places of the Internet boom years, where employees brainstormed the "next big thing," have yielded to formal, state-of-the-art conference centers, employee cafés and a prescribed number of informal meeting areas. "Like casual Fridays, casual meeting spaces only succeed when corporate cultures support them," says William Bouchey, design director of Mancini-Duffy, a noted New York-based architecture and interior design firm. Adds Dina Frank, president of Mancini-Duffy, "The new meeting facilities are prompted by a concern for security as well as renewed interest in defining clear boundaries."

- Amenity spaces: A happy consequence of smaller individual work stations is bigger and more varied employee amenities. How generous employers are with such amenities as cafeterias, daycare centers, fitness facilities, daylight and "green" design depends on such factors as work force demographics, costs and floor area. "The larger the project, the more a company can do for its employees," explains Juliette Lam, a senior principal of Hellmuth, Obata & Kassabaum, the much-honored, largest architecture firm in America. "An extensive day care center, often contracted to an accredited operator, is feasible for a suburban office. In an urban office day care will be for emergencies."

*Take this job*

Besides confronting economic competition, evolving information technologies and theories of business administration, organizations must also acknowledge the changing composition of office workers in developing office space. Women, minorities, working parents, rising Gen Xers and aging Baby Boomers are bringing different goals and attitudes to work. Flexible hours, shared work, hoteling and satellite offices are just some of the ways employers could adapt the workplace to respond.

"The first Boomers will be eligible for early retirement in 2007, when they reach 62," declares Christine Barber, director of workplace research for Knoll, a distinguished office furniture manufacturer with historic ties to the Bauhaus. "It could be a critical time for corporate America. Can employers continue to make the office more efficient when they may need a more pleasant environment to placate ambitious Gen Xers, who frequently want to be treated as stars? Or to dissuade experienced Boomers, many of whom are demoralized, from walking out and exacerbating the Baby Bust?"

Barber points out that many organizations now want to improve their operations by "branding" employees as well as workplaces, much as IBM did with its well-trained, neatly-groomed and highly-motivated work force in the postwar years. IBM set an impressive example in managing its human resources and corporate design—major elements of a winning corporate culture—en route to conquering the information technology industry. Will others follow in its steps? As the 21st century unfolds, there is no shortage of companies that want to be the next Microsoft, Citigroup or Procter & Gamble.

# Resources *

## ABN AMPC Plaza - Cafeteria
**Design Firm:** VOA Associates Incorporated
**Furniture:** Knoll
**Carpets & Flooring:** Bentley, Terrazzo
**Fabrics:** Knoll, Spinneybeck
**Lighting:** Color Kinetics, Eureka, Fiberstar, Focal Point, Louis Poulsen, Lucifer, Sonoma
**Ceilings:** Armstrong, Simplex, USG
**Wallcoverings:** Armourcoat, Benjamin Moore, Dupont, Imperial Woodworking, Scuffmaster
**General Contractors:** Turner Construction

## ABN AMPO Plaza - Conference & Training Center
**Design Firm:** VOA Associates Incorporated
**Furniture:** Davis, Herman Miller, Knoll, Luminaire, Nienkamper
**Carpets & Flooring:** Shaw, Terrazzo
**Fabrics:** Spinneybeck
**Lighting:** Eureka, Focal Point, Louis Poulsen, Reggiani
**Ceilings:** Armstrong
**Wallcoverings:** Benjamin Moore, Dupont, Imperial Woodworking, Zolatone
**General Contractors:** Power Construction Co.

## ABN AMPO Plaza - General Office Space
**Design Firm:** VOA Associates Incorporated
**Furniture:** Geiger, Herman Miller, Knoll, Luminaire, Nienkamper
**Carpets & Flooring:** Nora, Shaw, Stonecraft
**Fabrics:** KI, Pallas
**Lighting:** Focal Point
**Ceilings:** Armstrong
**Wallcoverings:** Benjamin Moore, Dupont, Imperial Woodworking, Zolatone
**General Contractors:** Power Construction Co.

## ABN AMPO Plaza - Retail Bank
**Design Firm:** VOA Associates Incorporated
**Furniture:** Geiger, Herman Miller, Luminaire
**Carpets & Flooring:** Masland, Shaw, Terrazzo
**Fabrics:** Maharam, Spinneybeck
**Lighting:** IO Lighting, Louis Poulsen
**Ceilings:** Armstrong
**Wallcoverings:** Benjamin Moore, Dupont
**General Contractors:** Turner Construction, SPD

## Abrams Capital
**Design Firm:** CBT/Childs Bertman Tseckares, Inc.
**Furniture:** Baker, Datesweiser, Elitis Mobilier, Eric Brand, Gerard, Lucien Rollin, Nienkamper, Promemoria
**Carpets & Flooring:** Hokanson, Karastan
**Fabrics:** Bergamo, Brunschwig & Fils, Clarence House, Larsen, Nancy Corzine
**Lighting:** Focal Point, Icon Group, Indy Lighting, Jiun Ho, Louis Poulsen, Metalux, McGuire, Neoray
**Ceilings:** Armstrong, Henry Calvin Fabrics
**Wallcoverings:** California Paints, Henry Calvin Fabrics, Garrett Woven Leather, Henry Calvin Fabrics, Pratt & Lambert, Sherwin Williams
**General Contractors:** Shawmut Design and Construction

## Absolut
**Design Firm:** Gensler
**Furniture:** Herman Miller, Knoll, Pucci, Unifor, Vitra, William Somerville, Zographos
**Carpets & Flooring:** Glen Eden, I.J. Peiser's Sons
**Wallcoverings:** Novawall
**General Contractors:** NTX Interiors

## Adams Street Partners
**Design Firm:** VOA Associates Incorporated
**Furniture:** HBF
**Carpets & Flooring:** Armstrong, Constantine
**Fabrics:** Donghia
**Lighting:** Nulite
**Ceilings:** USG
**Wallcoverings:** Benjamin Moore, Donghia
**General Contractors:** Clune Construction

## Allsteel Headquarters
**Design Firm:** Gensler
**Furniture:** Allsteel, Holly Hunt, Pottery Barn, Smith and

## Hawken
**Carpets & Flooring:** Lees
**Lighting:** Akari, Zumtobel Staff
**Wallcoverings:** ICI Paint
**General Contractors:** Knutson General Construction

## American College of Radiology
**Design Firm:** Meyer Associates, Inc.
**Furniture:** DiNardo Custom Woodworking, KI, Knoll, Nucraft, Sit on It
**Carpets & Flooring:** Amtico, Invision, Momentum
**Fabrics:** Bernhardt, Designtex, Pallas
**Lighting:** Lightolier
**Wallcoverings:** Eykon
**General Contractors:** D'Lauro & Rodgers

## American Red Cross
**Design Firm:** Griswold, Heckel & Kelly Associates, Inc. (GHK)
**Furniture:** Cooper, David Edward, Falcon, Haworth, ISE, Lowenstein, Paoli, Peter Pepper, Vecta, Versteel,
**Carpets & Flooring:** Armstrong, Atmosphere, Constantine, Dal Tile, Interface, Mannington, Mapei, Metropolitan, Milliken, Mondo, USA, Quarry Tile
**Fabrics:** Designtex, Haworth, Maharam, Pallas
**Lighting:** Bruck, Finelite, Lightolier, Zumtobel Staff
**Ceilings:** Armstrong
**Wallcoverings:** Duron, Kemlite, Korogard, Roppe, Wolf Gordon
**General Contractors:** Clark Construction

## Analytical Graphics
**Design Firm:** Meyer Associates, Inc.
**Furniture:** CCN International, Davis
**Carpets & Flooring:** Durkan, Milliken
**Fabrics:** ArcCom, Knoll
**Lighting:** Penn Lighting
**Wallcoverings:** Eykon
**General Contractors:** Turner Construction

## Austin Ventures
**Design Firm:** Susman Tisdale Gayle
**Furniture:** Brochsteins, Brueton, Casa Milano, Cleator, Creative Wood, HBF, ICF, Keilhauer, Kron, MDF, Minotti, Moltini, Moroso, Nienkamper, Office Specialty, Steelcase, Tuohy, Versteel
**Carpets & Flooring:** Karastan, Venice Art Terrazzo
**Ceilings:** Armstrong
**Wallcoverings:** Designtex, Monarch

## Baker Botts LLP
**Design Firm:** Gensler
**Furniture:** Brochstein's, Knoll
**Carpets & Flooring:** Bentley, Fritz Tile, Scott Group Rugs
**Fabrics:** Carnegie, Knoll, Spinneybeck, Unika Vaev
**Lighting:** Light Control, Lightolier, Neo-Ray
**Ceilings:** Armstrong, Eurospan
**Wallcoverings:** Kelly Moore Paint, Maharam
**General Contractors:** W.S. Bellows Construction Corp.

## Bank of America, 40 W. 57th Street
**Design Firm:** Nelson
**Furniture:** Brayton, Egan, Hamilton Sorter, Herman Miller, Keilhauer, Knoll, Modern Office Systems, Rialto Furniture
**Carpets & Flooring:** Ceramic Technics, Flexco, Johnsonite, Shaw, Toli Int'l
**Fabrics:** Bernhardt, Edelman Leather, Knoll, Pallas, Paul Brayton, Pollack, Spinneybeck, Unika Vaev
**Lighting:** CBL, Eureka, Kurt Versen, LiteControl, National, Zumtobel Staff
**Ceilings:** Armstrong, Decoustics, Eurospan, Newmat
**Wallcoverings:** Benjamin Moore, Ceramic Techniques, Designtex, Koroseal, Maharam, Pallas, Stone Source, Unika Vaev, Wolf Gordon
**General Contractors:** Structure Tone, Inc.

## Bank of Smithtown
**Design Firm:** Mojo Stumer Architects
**Furniture:** Steelcase
**Carpets & Flooring:** A&G Mastercraft, AMI Marble, Mohawk
**Fabrics:** Designtex
**Lighting:** Beta-Calco, Indy Lighting, Lite-Tech, WAC
**Ceilings:** Armstrong

## Wallcoverings: Benjamin Moore, JM Lynne
**General Contractors:** Horan Construction

## Barefoot Books
**Design Firm:** Margulies & Associates
**Carpets & Flooring:** Atlas
**Fabrics:** Knoll
**Lighting:** 2 Thousand Degrees
**Wallcoverings:** Benjamin Moore
**General Contractors:** Walter Wetstone Builders

## Bear Sterns and Company Corporate Headquarters
**Design Firm:** Gerner Kronick + Valcarcel, Architects, PC
**Furniture:** Baker, Knoll
**Carpets & Flooring:** Durkan, Port Morris Tile & Marble
**Lighting:** Nessen
**Ceilings:** Armstrong
**Wallcoverings:** Vescom
**General Contractors:** Frank Sciame Construction

## The Berwind Group
**Design Firm:** Meyer Associates, Inc.
**Furniture:** CCN International, Davis, Teknion
**Carpets & Flooring:** Monterrey
**Fabrics:** ArcCom, Garrett Leather, Maharam
**Lighting:** Focal Point
**Wallcoverings:** Benjamin Moore
**General Contractors:** Clemens Construction

## Beted Reserves & Trading
**Design Firm:** OWP/P
**Furniture:** FCI, Herman Miller, Knoll
**Carpets & Flooring:** Interface, Lonseal
**Fabrics:** Knoll, Spinneybeck
**Lighting:** Elliptipar, Focal Point, Lightolier, Lithonia, Tech Lighting
**Ceilings:** USG
**Wallcoverings:** Benjamin Moore, Scuffmaster
**General Contractors:** Alps Construction, Inc.

## Browr Rudnick
**Design Firm:** CBT/Childs Bertman Tseckares, Inc.
**Furniture:** B&B Italia, Herman Miller, ICF, Knoll, Neinkamper
**Carpets & Flooring:** Glen Eden, Karastan, Prince Street
**Fabrics:** Knoll, Maharam, Spinneybeck
**Lighting:** Columbia, Edison Price, Elliptipar, Louis Poulsen
**Ceilings:** Armstrong, Ecophon
**Wallcoverings:** Benjamin Moore, IZIT Leather Panels
**General Contractors:** Turner Construction

## Broadjump
**Design Firm:** Susman Tisdale Gayle
**Furniture:** K&J Woodworks, Steelcase
**Carpets & Flooring:** Prince Street, Shaw
**Fabrics:** Formica, Nevamar, Wilsonart
**Lighting:** Louis Poulsen, Ness America, Peerless, Shaper
**Wallcoverings:** Benjamin Moore
**General Contractors:** DPR Construction

## Carney Badley
**Design Firm:** JPC Architects
**Furniture:** MEI Office Interiors
**Carpets & Flooring:** Armstrong, Atlas, Oregon Tile & Marble
**Fabrics:** Formica, Nevamar, Wilsonart
**Lighting:** Lightolier
**Ceilings:** Armstrong
**Wallcoverings:** Benjamin Moore
**General Contractors:** McCarthy Construction

## Caruso
**Design Firm:** Wolcott Architecture Interiors
**Furniture:** Wavell Huber
**Fabrics:** Donghai, Jim Thompson, J. Robert Scott
**Lighting:** Lithonia, Lucifer
**Ceilings:** Decoustics
**General Contractors:** Nexus Construction

**CB Richard Ellis**
**Design Firm:** Perkins Eastman Architects
**Furniture:** Bernhardt, Datesweiser, Knoll, Lowenstein
**Carpets & Flooring:** Armstrong, Mohawk, Shaw
**Fabrics:** ArcCom
**Lighting:** Contech, Finelite, Lightolier
**Ceilings:** Armstrong
**Wallcoverings:** Benjamin Moore, Scuffmaster
**General Contractors:** W&M Construction

**Christensen, Miller, Fink, Jacobs, Glaser, Weil & Shapiro**
**Design Firm:** Aref Associates
**Furniture:** Knoll, Vitra
**Carpets & Flooring:** Karastan
**Fabrics:** Knoll, Maharam
**Lighting:** Baldinger, Lightolier
**Ceilings:** Armstrong, USG
**Wallcoverings:** Frazee, Knoll
**General Contractors:** Environmental Contracting Corporation

**Clark Thomas & Winters**
**Design Firm:** Susman Tisdale Gayle
**Furniture:** Allsteel, Bernhardt, Bright, Creative Wood, Gordon International, Harter, HBF, LaZBoy, Martin Brattrud, Nienkamper, Novikoff, Office Specialty, Spacesaver, Sit On It, Tuohy, Versteel, Watson
**Carpets & Flooring:** Constantine, Durkan, Stone Solutions
**Fabrics:** Carnegie
**Ceilings:** Armstrong
**Wallcoverings:** Carnegie, ICI

**Clifford Chance US LLP**
**Design Firm:** AREA
**Furniture:** Holly Hunt, Knoll, Vitra
**Carpets & Flooring:** Constantine
**Fabrics:** Knoll, Spinneybeck
**Lighting:** Legion, Portfolio
**Ceilings:** Armstrong
**Wallcoverings:** Carnegie, Pratt & Lambert
**General Contractors:** Hathaway Dinwiddie Construction

**Comedy Central**
**Design Firm:** Gerner Kronick + Valcarcel, Architects, PC
**Furniture:** Bernhardt, Cappellini, Davis, Geiger, Halcon, Harter, HBF, Herman Miller, ICF, Keilhauer, Knoll, Metro, Steelcase, Vecta
**Carpets & Flooring:** Bentley, Daltile, Dex-O-Tex, Forbo, Graniti Fiandre, Interface, Johnsonite, Marley Floors, Monterey, Prince Street, Roppe
**Lighting:** Elliptipar, Flos, Forum, Legion, Lightolier, Litelab, Rambusch, RSA
**Ceilings:** Armstrong
**Wallcoverings:** Benjamin Moore, Buchtal Tile, Dupont, JM Lynne
**General Contractors:** Lehr Construction Corp.

**Constellation**
**Design Firm:** Griswold, Heckel & Kelly Associates, Inc. (GHK)
**Furniture:** David Edward, HBF, Herman Miller, Meridian, Patella, Steelcase, Teknion
**Carpets & Flooring:** Karastan, Mannington, Masland, Monterey, Shaw, Stone Source, Toli
**Fabrics:** ArcCom, Designtex, Maharam, Momentum, Sina Pearson
**Lighting:** Concealite, Davis Muller, Daybrite, Edison Price, Focal Point, Forecast, Lightolier, Lucifer, McPhilben, Winona Lighting
**Ceilings:** Decoustics, Ecophon, USG
**Wallcoverings:** Designtex, Duron, JM Lynne
**General Contractors:** Whiting Turner

**Corbis**
**Design Firm:** JPC Architects
**Furniture:** Herman Miller
**Carpets & Flooring:** Atlas, Pacific Crest Mills
**Fabrics:** Herman Miller
**Lighting:** Contech
**Ceilings:** Armstrong
**Wallcoverings:** Benjamin Moore, Sherwin Williams, Xorel
**General Contractors:** Turner Construction

**Credit Suisse**
**Design Firm:** Leotta Designers Inc.
**Furniture:** Cleator, Steelcase
**Carpets & Flooring:** Constantine, Keys Granite
**Fabrics:** Brentano
**Lighting:** Leucos
**Ceilings:** Armstrong
**Wallcoverings:** Benjamin Moore, Maharam
**General Contractors:** Pavarini

**Dade Paper**
**Design Firm:** Leotta Designers Inc.
**Furniture:** Bernhardt, Teknion
**Carpets & Flooring:** Atlas, Keys Granite
**Fabrics:** Bernhardt, Knoll
**Lighting:** Boyd
**Ceilings:** Armstrong
**Wallcoverings:** Benjamin Moore, Blumenthal, Carnegie, JM Lynne, Maharam, National, Vicoryl
**General Contractors:** Itasca

**Dancker Sellen & Douglas**
**Design Firm:** Francis Cauffman Foley Hoffmann, Architects Ltd.
**Furniture:** Steelcase
**Carpets & Flooring:** Armstrong, Interface, Lees, Milliken, Shaw
**Fabrics:** Designtex
**Lighting:** Lightolier
**Wallcoverings:** Benjamin Moore, Zolatone
**General Contractors:** Dancker Sellen & Douglas

**Dan Kettener Riley Wright & Rybalt LLP**
**Design Firm:** Oliver Design Group
**Furniture:** Donghia
**Carpets & Flooring:** Amtico, Armstrong, Azrock, Bentley, Lees, Monterey, Stone Design
**Fabrics:** Jhane Barnes
**Lighting:** Ardec Lighting, Artemide, Corelite, Halo, Juno, Kurt Versen, Litecontrol, Lithonia, Metalux, Ron Rezek
**Ceilings:** Armstrong, Decoustico
**Wallcoverings:** Benjamin Moore, Dupont, ICI, Innovation, Jhane Barnes, JM Lynne, Zolatone
**General Contractors:** Fred Olivieri Construction Co.

**The Dannon Company**
**Design Firm:** Perkins Eastman Architects
**Furniture:** Bernhardt, Brayton, Herman Miller, Nienkamper, Unifor, Zenith
**Carpets & Flooring:** Atlas, Stone Source
**Fabrics:** Bernhardt, Maharam
**Lighting:** Lightolier, LSC
**Ceilings:** Armstrong
**Wallcoverings:** Benjamin Moore, Walltalkers, Wolf Gordon
**General Contractors:** Bovis Land Lease

**Delcordia Technologies**
**Design Firm:** Francis Cauffman Foley Hoffmann, Architects Ltd.
**Furniture:** Haworth
**Carpets & Flooring:** Shaw
**Fabrics:** Designtex
**Lighting:** Cooper, Eureka, Neoray
**Ceilings:** USG
**Wallcoverings:** Benjamin Moore, Designtex
**General Contractors:** Sordoni / Skansa

**Deloitte Global Headquarters**
**Design Firm:** Ted Moudis Associates
**Furniture:** Steelcase, Stow Davis
**Carpets & Flooring:** Constantine, Stone Source, Worldwide Stone
**Fabrics:** Brunschwig & Fils, HBF, Yoma
**Lighting:** Boyd, Mark Lighting
**Ceilings:** Armstrong
**Wallcoverings:** Benjamin Moore, Carnegie, Maharam
**General Contractors:** Structure Tone, Inc.

**D-Parture Spa**
**Design Firm:** Silvester + Tafuro, Inc.
**Furniture:** Salon Interiors
**Carpets & Flooring:** Ardex, Bruce Hardwood Floors
**Fabrics:** Knoll

**Lighting:** Color Kinetics, CU Lighting, Lightolier, Zumtobel Staff
**Ceilings:** Armstrong
**Wallcoverings:** Benjamin Moore, Wilsonart

**Discount Tire**
**Design Firm:** McCarthy Nordburg
**Furniture:** Knoll
**Carpets & Flooring:** Bentley, Durkan, Paris Ceramics
**Fabrics:** Whisper Walls
**Lighting:** Creative Designs in Lighting, R.C. Lurie, Roberts Step-Lite Systems
**Ceilings:** Whisper Walls
**Wallcoverings:** Benjamin Moore
**General Contractors:** Opus West Construction Corp.

**1818 Market Street**
**Design Firm:** Meyer Associates, Inc.
**Carpets & Flooring:** Coldsprings Granite Company
**Fabrics:** Designtex
**Lighting:** Lighting Design Collaborative
**Wallcoverings:** MDC

**EMI Recorded Music**
**Design Firm:** Mancini-Duffy
**Furniture:** Design Link, HBF, Herman Miller, Holly Hunt, Knoll, Troy Contract
**Carpets & Flooring:** Armstrong, Architectural Systems, Bentley, Interface, Prince Street
**Fabrics:** Bellinger, Carnegie, Forbo, Holly Hunt, IKG Industries, Maharam, Pollack, Unika Vaev, Wolf Gordon
**Lighting:** Artemide, Kurt Versen, Lightolier, Linear, Zumtobel Staff
**Ceilings:** Armstrong
**Wallcoverings:** Benjamin Moore, Vitruv
**General Contractors:** Lehr Construction Company

**FactSet Headquarters**
**Design Firm:** Roger Ferris & Partners
**Furniture:** Geiger, Knoll, Neinkamper, Steelcase
**Carpets & Flooring:** Forbo, Monterey
**Fabrics:** Bernhardt, Designtex, Spinneybeck
**Lighting:** Alkco, Kurt Versen, Linear, Zumtobel Staff
**Ceilings:** Armstrong, Ecophon
**Wallcoverings:** Donald Kaufman, Maharam
**General Contractors:** A.D.P. Construction Services

**First Marblehead**
**Design Firm:** CBT/Childs Bertman Tseckares, Inc.
**Furniture:** B&B Italia, Baker, Bernhardt, Custom Millwork Furniture, Flexform, Herman Miller, Keilhauer, Knoll, Poltrona Frau, Promemoria, Ralph Pucci
**Carpets & Flooring:** Bloomsburg, Eurotex, Stark Carpet
**Fabrics:** Bergamo, Bernhardt, Edelman Leather, Gretchen Bellinger, Knoll, Kvadrat, Larsen, Nancy Corzine, Poltrona Frau Leather
**Lighting:** BSA, Columbia, Edison Price, Hermes, Indy Lighting, Louis Poulsen, Palmer Hargrave, Peerless, Quiet Ceiling, Ralph Pucci
**Ceilings:** Armstrong, Knoll Textiles
**Wallcoverings:** Pratt & Lambert, Schreuder Paint
**General Contractors:** Shawmut Design and Construction

**Ford, Dagenham, Diesel Design Centre, UK**
**Design Firm:** HOK International Limited (London, UK)
**Furniture:** Steelcase
**Carpets & Flooring:** Amtico, Armstrong, Freudenberg, Interface
**Fabrics:** Steelcase
**Lighting:** Philips
**Ceilings:** British Gypsum, SAS International
**Wallcoverings:** Delux Paint, Polyreg Plastic
**General Contractors:** SDC Builders Ltd.

**Fuji Photo Film U.S.A.**
**Design Firm:** Perkins Eastman Architects
**Furniture:** Davis, Keilhauer, Tuohy, Unifor
**Carpets & Flooring:** Constantine, Shaw
**Fabrics:** Anzea, Carnegie, Designtex, Maharam, Pollack, Xorel
**Lighting:** Cooper Lighting, Metalux, Zumtobel Staff
**Ceilings:** Armstrong
**Wallcoverings:** Benjamin Moore, Gilford, Scuffmaster

# WOOD SOLUTIONS FOR BUSINESS ENVIRONMENTS

*project profile*

location: Detroit, Michigan
architect: Ford & Earl
photography: Glen Calvin Moon
product: modified Kubit and FOUNDATION

**INTERNATIONAL**

315 • 789 • 4400
www.ccninternational.com

**General Contractors:** CW Brown, Inc.

**G4 Media**
**Design Firm:** Aref Associates
**Furniture:** Herman Miller, Knoll, Vitra
**Carpets & Flooring:** Milliken
**Fabrics:** Knoll, Maharam
**Lighting:** Lightolier, Lithonia
**Ceilings:** Armstrong, Artemide, Eureka, Flos, Foscarini, Luce, Murano Due, USG
**Wallcoverings:** Frazee, ICI, Knoll
**General Contractors:** Taslimi Construction Company

**Gibson, Dunn & Crutcher**
**Design Firm:** Aref & Associates
**Furniture:** HBF, Knoll
**Carpets & Flooring:** Karastan
**Fabrics:** ArcCom, Designtex, Knoll
**Lighting:** Baldinger, Boyd, Eureka, Lightolier
**Ceilings:** Armstrong, USG
**General Contractors:** Taslimi Construction Company

**Glaxo Smith Kline**
**Design Firm:** Francis Cauffman Foley Hoffmann, Architects Ltd.
**Furniture:** Steelcase
**Carpets & Flooring:** Lees
**Fabrics:** Designtex, Paul Bratton
**Lighting:** Focal Point, Lithonia
**Ceilings:** Armstrong
**Wallcoverings:** Designtex, Knoll
**General Contractors:** Norwood

**Goulston & Storrs, P.C.**
**Design Firm:** CBT/Childs Bertman Tseckares, Inc.
**Furniture:** Datesweiser, Geiger, Knoll
**Carpets & Flooring:** Bentley, Bloomsburg
**Fabrics:** Donghia, Edelman Leather, Knoll
**Lighting:** Focal Point
**Ceilings:** Armstrong
**Wallcoverings:** Benjamin Moore, Designtex, Edelman Leather
**General Contractors:** Shawmut Design and Construction

**Gray Plant Moog Corporate Offices**
**Design Firm:** Ellerbe Becket, Inc.
**Furniture:** Brayton, Cartwright, Epic, Harter, HBF, ICF, Keilhauer, Metro, Steelcase
**Carpets & Flooring:** Graniti Fiandre, Masland, TilexDesign
**Fabrics:** Brayton, Designtex, Knoll, Maharam, Spinneybeck
**Lighting:** Capri, Fad Lighting, Focal Point, LBL, Leucos, Lightolier, Lithonia, Neoray, Reggiani, Tanslite
**Ceilings:** USG
**Wallcoverings:** Benjamin Moore, Innovations, JM Lynne, Knoll, Maharam, Sherwin Williams, Wolf Gordon
**General Contractors:** Greiner Construction

**Gust Rosenfeld**
**Design Firm:** McCarthy Nordburg
**Furniture:** KP Mfg, SMED
**Carpets & Flooring:** Designweave, Prince Street
**Fabrics:** Designtex, Knoll, Paul Brayton
**Lighting:** Energie, Eureka, Lithonia
**Ceilings:** USG
**Wallcoverings:** Dunn Edwards, Knoll
**General Contractors:** Opus West Construction

**Guy Carpenter, New York**
**Design Firm:** Hellmuth, Obata + Kassabaum, P.C.
**Furniture:** Bernhardt, Steelcase, Vecta
**Carpets & Flooring:** Milliken, Monterey, Stone Source
**Fabrics:** Carnegie, Designtex, Maharam, Spinneybeck, Unika Vaev
**Lighting:** BSA, Lightolier, Translite
**Ceilings:** Armstrong
**Wallcoverings:** Benjamin Moore
**General Contractors:** Structure Tone

**Harris Trust Bank at the Biltmore**
**Design Firm:** McCarthy Nordburg
**Furniture:** Bernhardt, David Edwards, Loewenstein, Versteel
**Carpets & Flooring:** Armstrong, AZ Tile, Bentley, Interface, Prince Street, Mannington, S. Bolyu

**Fabrics:** Designtex, Knoll, Liz Jordan Hall, Maharam, Unika Vaev
**Wallcoverings:** Frazee
**General Contractors:** C3 Construction

**Haworth Merchandise Mart Showroom**
**Design Firm:** Perkins + Will
**Furniture:** Haworth
**Carpets & Flooring:** Interface, Shaw
**Fabrics:** Haworth
**Lighting:** Axis, Kurt Versen
**Ceilings:** Ecophon, Rulon
**Wallcoverings:** Benjamin Moore, Haworth

**Hays Companies**
**Design Firm:** Ellerbe Beckett, Inc.
**Furniture:** Bernhardt, Cramer, Davis, Falcon, HBF, Johnson, Steelcase, Teknion, Tuohy
**Carpets & Flooring:** Bentley, Constantine, Gladino Limestone, Mannington, Masland, Prince Street, Rossi USA
**Fabrics:** Designtex, HBF, Luna
Sina Pearson, Teknion
**Lighting:** Foscarini, Illuminating Experiences, Leucos, Lightolier, Lucifer, Tech Lighting
**Ceilings:** Celotex, Hunter Douglas
**Wallcoverings:** Benjamin Moore, Knoll, Maharam
**General Contractors:** RJM Construction

**Herman Miller Los Angeles Design Center**
**Design Firm:** AREA
**Furniture:** Herman Miller
**Carpets & Flooring:** Bentley, Chilewich, Prince Street
**Fabrics:** Herman Miller
**Lighting:** Legion, Portfolio
**Ceilings:** Barisol
**Wallcoverings:** Carnegie, Fabric-Trak, Pratt & Lambert, Xorel
Window Treatments: Mechoshade
**General Contractors:** Howard Building Corporation

**Hernan's Headquarters**
**Design Firm:** Oliver Design Group
**Furniture:** Haworth, Inscape, Keilhauer, Vecta, Versteel
**Fabrics:** Anzea, Designtex
**Lighting:** Corelite, Juno, Litecontrol, Lithonia
**Ceilings:** Armstrong, USG
**Wallcoverings:** Benjamin Moore, ICI, Scuffmaster
**General Contractors:** Infinity Construction Co.

**H. Hendy Associates Corporate Headquarters**
**Design Firm:** H. Hendy Associates
**Furniture:** Geiger, Herman Miller, Wavell Huber Custom
**Carpets & Flooring:** Bolyu, Permagrain, Prince Street, Shaw
**Fabrics:** Luna
**Lighting:** Bruck, Del Ray, Finelite, Tango, Wila
**Ceilings:** Armstrong
**Wallcoverings:** Innovation, Maharam, Zolatone
**General Contractors:** Turelk

**Holideck**
**Design Firm:** Silvester + Tafuro, Inc.
**Furniture:** Artifort, Johnson, Steelcase, Wilkahn
**Fabrics:** Kuadrat
**Lighting:** Davey, Flos, Foscarini
**Ceilings:** SAS

**Houlihan Lokey**
**Design Firm:** Wolcott Architecture Interiors
**Furniture:** Brayton, Giesberger
**Carpets & Flooring:** Constantine
**Fabrics:** Knoll, Maharam
**Lighting:** Lithonia
**Wallcoverings:** Wolf-Gordon
**General Contractors:** Nexus Construction

**Hudson Health Campus**
**Design Firm:** Nelson
**Furniture:** Allsteel, Cabot Wrenn, David Edward, Haworth, Integra, KI, Nemschoff, Sit On It
**Carpets & Flooring:** American Olean, Armstrong, Atlas, J&J, Mannington, Patcraft
**Fabrics:** ArcCom, Architex, Carnegie, Designtex, Gilford, Knoll,

Liz Jordan Hill, Maharam, One Plus One, Pallas, Paul Bratton, Schumacher, Sina Pearson
**Lighting:** Columbia, DA-C, ELP, Eureka, Forum, Gammalux, Lithonia, Linear Lighting, Metalumen, Predenthal, Prescolite, Spaulding, Williams
**Ceilings:** Armstrong
**Wallcoverings:** CS Group, JM Lynne, Lentex, Maharam, MDC, Sherwin Williams, Verga, Wolf Gordon
**General Contractors:** Mortenson

**Hudson News Euro Cafe**
**Design Firm:** Silvester + Tafuro, Inc.
**Furniture:** Design Within Reach
**Carpets & Flooring:** American Olean
**Fabrics:** Wilsonart
**Lighting:** BK, George Kovacs, Halo, LBL, Metalux, Tech Lighting
**Ceilings:** Armstrong
**Wallcoverings:** Benjamin Moore

**Huron Consulting Group**
**Design Firm:** Griswold, Heckel & Kelly Associates, Inc. (GHK)
**Furniture:** Allsteel, Bernhardt, Brayton, Bright, Coach, FCI, Gunlocke, HBF, Keilhauer, Leland, Source International
**Carpets & Flooring:** Bentley, Forbo, Interface, Landis
**Fabrics:** ArcCom, Knoll, Luna, Maharam, Pallas, Spinneybeck
**Lighting:** Artemide, Lighting Services, Lightolier, Louis Poulsen, Prudential
**Ceilings:** Armstrong
**Wallcoverings:** Benjamin Moore, ICI, Knoll, Maharam, Scuffmaster
**General Contractors:** Leopardo Companies, Inc.

**ICAP North America, Inc.**
**Design Firm:** Ted Moudis Associates
**Furniture:** Brayton, Cabot Wren, Davis, Geiger, Herman Miller, ICF, Keilhauer, Knoll, Lacour, Nienkamper, Vccta
**Carpets & Flooring:** Amtico, Congoleum, Constantine, Forbo, Interface, Lonseal, Shaw, Stone Source
**Fabrics:** Bernhardt, Designtex, HBF, Knoll
**Lighting:** Kurt Versen, Linear
**Ceilings:** Armstrong
**Wallcoverings:** Ann Sacks, Benjamin Moore, JM Lynne, Lanark, Wolf Gordon
**General Contractors:** Structure Tone, Inc.

**Intercontinental Developers Inc.**
**Design Firm:** Margulies & Associates
**Furniture:** Teknion
**Carpets & Flooring:** Mannington, Masland, Monterey
**Fabrics:** Luna, Maharam
**Lighting:** Belfer, Kim Lighting, Lightolier, Luceplan, Techlighting
**Ceilings:** Armstrong
**Wallcoverings:** ICI, Pallas
**General Contractors:** Intercontinental Developers Inc.

**JAFCO Ventures**
**Design Firm:** Margulies & Associates
**Furniture:** Kimball
**Carpets & Flooring:** Forbo, Shaw
**Fabrics:** Bernhardt, Spinneybeck
**Lighting:** Columbia, Lightolier, Techlighting
**Ceilings:** USG
**Wallcoverings:** Benjamin Moore, Unika Vaev
**General Contractors:** Shawmut Design & Construction

**JMB**
**Design Firm:** OWP/P
**Furniture:** Bright, HBF
**Carpets & Flooring:** Karastan, Monterrey
**Fabrics:** Pollack
**Lighting:** Edison Price, Kurt Versen, Lightolier, Lucifer, Portfolio, Starfire
**Ceilings:** Parenti & Rafaelli, USG
**Wallcoverings:** Benjamin Moore, Keleen Leathers
**General Contractors:** ISI Construction

**Kilroy Realty Corporation**
**Design Firm:** Aref & Associates
**Furniture:** Tuohy
**Carpets & Flooring:** Armstrong, Interface, Milliken
**Fabrics:** Spinneybeck

**Lighting:** Flos, Jammar, Louis Poulsen
**Ceilings:** USG
**Wallcoverings:** Frazee, Knoll
**General Contractors:** Turelk, Inc.

The Marketing Store
**Design Firm:** Gary Lee Partners
**Furniture:** Knoll, Vitra
**Carpets & Flooring:** Shaw
**Fabrics:** Knoll, Maharam
**Lighting:** Focal Point, Lightolier
**Ceilings:** USG
**Wallcoverings:** Benjamin Moore, Pantone
**General Contractors:** Turner Construction

MacQuarie Capital Partners LLC
**Design Firm:** Gary Lee Partners
**Furniture:** Herman Miller, Knoll, Unifor, Zobraphos
**Carpets & Flooring:** Armstrong, Karastan
**Fabrics:** Herman Miller, Spinneybeck
**Lighting:** Boyd/Lightspace, Lightolier, Peerless
**Ceilings:** Armstrong, Hunter Douglas, USG
**Wallcoverings:** Benjamin Moore
**General Contractors:** Clune Construction Inc.

A Major Financial Institution - Irvine, Cal.
**Design Firm:** H. Hendy Associates
**Furniture:** Geiger, Herman Miller
**Carpets & Flooring:** Monterey
**Fabrics:** Jhane Barnes, Knoll, Maharam, Pollack, Unika Vaev
**Lighting:** Atmosphere, Boyd
**Ceilings:** Armstrong
**Wallcoverings:** Maharam, Zolatone
**General Contractors:** Turelk

A Major Financial Institution - Rolling Meadows, Ill.
**Design Firm:** H. Hendy Associates
**Furniture:** Geiger, Herman Miller
**Carpets & Flooring:** Shaw
**Fabrics:** HBF, Jhane Barnes, Luna
**Lighting:** Lithonia, Winona
**Ceilings:** Armstrong
**Wallcoverings:** Zolatone
**General Contractors:** Pepper Construction

A Major International Private Bank
**Design Firm:** Leotta Designers Inc.
**Furniture:** HBF, Knoll, Morrison Furniture System
**Carpets & Flooring:** Armstrong, Atlas, Keys Granite
**Fabrics:** Unika Vaev
**Lighting:** Leucos
**Ceilings:** Armstrong
**Wallcoverings:** Maharam
**General Contractors:** Itasca

The Marketing Store
**Design Firm:** Gary Lee Partners
**Furniture:** Knoll, Vitra
**Carpets & Flooring:** Shaw
**Fabrics:** Knoll, Maharam
**Lighting:** Focal Point, Lightolier
**Ceilings:** USG
**Wallcoverings:** Benjamin Moore, Pantone
**General Contractors:** Turner Construction

McKinsey & Co.
**Design Firm:** Oliver Design Groupp
**Furniture:** HBF, Herman Miller, Horizon, Metropolitan, Steelcase, Vecta
**Carpets & Flooring:** Atlas, Constantine, Forbo, Mannington
**Fabrics:** Anzea, ArcCom, Brayton International, Designtex, Knoll, Maharam, Momentum, Pallas, Paul Brayton, Spinneybeck, Unika Vaev
**Lighting:** Atkco, Danalite, Eliptipar, Energie, Focal Point, Halo, Italianaluce, Ledalite, Leucos, Lucifer, Metalux, Shop Kit, Tech Lighting
**Ceilings:** Armstrong, USG
**Wallcoverings:** Allusion, Benjamin Moore, Guilford, ICI, Knoll, Maharam, MDC, Oceanside Glass Tile, PPG, Scuffmaster, Symphony
**General Contractors:** Turner Construction Co.

McNeil Consumer & Specialty Pharmaceuticals
**Design Firm:** Francis Cauffman Foley Hoffmann Architects Ltd.
**Furniture:** Steelcase
**Carpets & Flooring:** Interface
**Fabrics:** Designtex
**Ceilings:** USG
**Wallcoverings:** Benjamin Moore, Designtex, Maharam, Sherwin Williams
**General Contractors:** W.H. Drayton & Company

MedImmune, Inc. Research and Administration Headquarters
**Design Firm:** Hellmuth, Obata + Kassabaum, P.C.
**Furniture:** David Edward, Herman Miller, Kimball
**Carpets & Flooring:** Prince Street
**Fabrics:** Deepa, Luna, Spinneybeck
**Lighting:** Erco, Kurt Versen, Lightolier, Selux
**Ceilings:** Armstrong
**Wallcoverings:** Benjamin Moore, Duron
**General Contractors:** Hitt Contracting, Inc.

Mercedes Benz Showroom
**Design Firm:** Gerner Kronick + Valcarcel, Architects, PC
**Furniture:** Cappellini, Cassina, Stylex
**Carpets & Flooring:** Lees, Wilkstone
**Lighting:** Johnson Schwinghammer Lighting Design
**Ceilings:** Barrisol Stretch Ceilings
**Wallcoverings:** Benjamin Moore, Venetial Plaster
**General Contractors:** Lehr Construction Corp.

Mojo Stumer Design Studio
**Design Firm:** Mojo Stumer Architects
**Furniture:** Knoll
**Carpets & Flooring:** Associated Marble, Country Carpets
**Fabrics:** Knoll
**Lighting:** Lighting Collaborative, Lightolier
**Ceilings:** Armstrong
**Wallcoverings:** Benjamin Moore
**General Contractors:** MSA

M2L
**Design Firm:** Gerner Kronick + Valcarcel, Architects, PC
**Furniture:** M2L
**Carpets & Flooring:** Rudy Art Glass
**Lighting:** Elliptipar
**Wallcoverings:** Benjamin Moore
**General Contractors:** NTD Construction

New York Tolerance Center
**Design Firm:** NBBJ
**Furniture:** American Seating, Gordon International, Jarrett Woodworking, Midstate Expositions, Vitra
**Carpets & Flooring:** Interface
**Fabrics:** Jhane Barnes, Knoll
**Lighting:** Lightolier, Stonco Lighting
**Ceilings:** Armstrong, Formica
**Wallcoverings:** Midstate Expositions
**General Contractors:** Lehr Construction

Northwest Community Hospital Cafeteria
**Design Firm:** OWP/P
**Furniture:** Epic, Knoll, Nevins
**Carpets & Flooring:** Cavetti, Collins & Aikman
**Fabrics:** Pallas
**Ceilings:** Armstrong
**Wallcoverings:** JC Licht
**General Contractors:** Power Construction Co.

1250 Broadway Lobby
**Design Firm:** Mancini-Duffy
**Furniture:** S&G Woodworking
**Carpets & Flooring:** Stone Source
**Lighting:** Kurt Versen
**Wallcoverings:** Novo Arts (mural)
**General Contractors:** Vanguard Construction & Development Co., Inc.

Ottawa University
**Design Firm:** McCarthy Nordburg
**Furniture:** HON, National
**Carpets & Flooring:** J&J Commercial, Monterey
**Fabrics:** Architex, Knoll, National

**Wallcoverings:** Koroseal, Maharam, Versa
**General Contractors:** Stevens Leinweber

Quadriga Asset Management
**Design Firm:** Griswold, Heckel & Kelly Associates, Inc. (GHK)
**Furniture:** Davis, Eurotech, Kimball
**Carpets & Flooring:** Armstrong, Dal Tile, Monterey, Wilsonart
**Lighting:** Del Ray, Eureka, Focal Point
**Ceilings:** Armstrong, Chicago Metallic Corp.
**Wallcoverings:** Benjamin Moore, ICI, Scuffmaster, Wolf Gordon
**General Contractors:** Interior Construction Group (ICG)

Paul Hastings New York
**Design Firm:** DMJM Rottet
**Furniture:** Bernhardt, Martin Bratrud, Minotti, Vitra
**Carpets & Flooring:** Bentley, Constantine, Prince Street
**Fabrics:** Bernhardt, Edelman Leather, Kravdet, Maharam
**Lighting:** Fisher Marantz Stone
**Ceilings:** USG
**Wallcoverings:** Benjamin Moore, Designtex, Knoll, Pratt & Lambert
**General Contractors:** Plaza Construction

Payton Construction
**Design Firm:** Margulies & Associates
**Carpets & Flooring:** Armstrong, Atlas
**Ceilings:** Tectum Acoustical Panels, USG
**Wallcoverings:** Designtex, ICI
**General Contractors:** Payton Construction

PepsiAmericas Executive Offices
**Design Firm:** Ellerbe Becket, Inc.
**Furniture:** Bernhardt, Davis, Halcon, Haworth, HBF, Krug, Reinhard, Tuohy
**Carpets & Flooring:** Bentley, Kate-Lo Tile, Landis Marble, Midwest Tile, Marble & Granite
**Fabrics:** ArcCom, Architex, Cortina, Designtex, Jhane Barnes, Luna, Maharam, Sina Pearson, Unika Vaev
**Lighting:** Belfer, Capri, Hera, Kurt Versen, Leucas, Lightolier
**Wallcoverings:** Benjamin Moore, Blumenthal, Carnegie, Hirschfield's, Maharam, Pollack, Scuffmaster
**General Contractors:** United Properties

Reed Elsevier
**Design Firm:** Mancini-Duffy
**Furniture:** Allstec, Datesweiser, Gunlocke, HBF, Herman Miller, ICF, Knoll
**Carpets & Flooring:** Atlas, Bloomsburg
**Fabrics:** Carnegie, Designtex, Maharam
**Lighting:** Ar-Lite, Artemide, Day Brite, Flos, Kurt Versen, Linear
**Ceilings:** Armstrong
**Wallcoverings:** Benjamin Moore, Carnegie, Forbo, Vitruv
**General Contractors:** J.T. Megan & Sons

Reed Smith LLP
**Design Firm:** AREA
**Furniture:** Diva, Eppink, Knoll, Martin Brattrud, Vitra
**Carpets & Flooring:** Constantine
**Fabrics:** Knoll, Sina Pearson
**Lighting:** Halo, Legion
**Ceilings:** Armstrong
**Wallcoverings:** Carnegie, Pratt & Lambert
**General Contractors:** Howard Building Corporation

The Ritz-Carlton Hotel Company, L.I.C.
**Design Firm:** Mancini-Duffy
**Furniture:** Dossier & Craftwood, Knoll
**Carpets & Flooring:** Potomac
**Fabrics:** Direct Path
**Ceilings:** C&C
**Wallcoverings:** Direct Path, Sea Wallcoverings
**General Contractors:** Rand Construction Corporation

Sabre Corporate Offices
**Design Firm:** Silvester + Tafuro, Inc.
**Furniture:** Herman Miller, Wilkhahn
**Carpets & Flooring:** Amtico, Interface, Mannington
**Fabrics:** Hartley, Kuadrat
**Lighting:** MEM, Reggiani
**Ceilings:** SAS

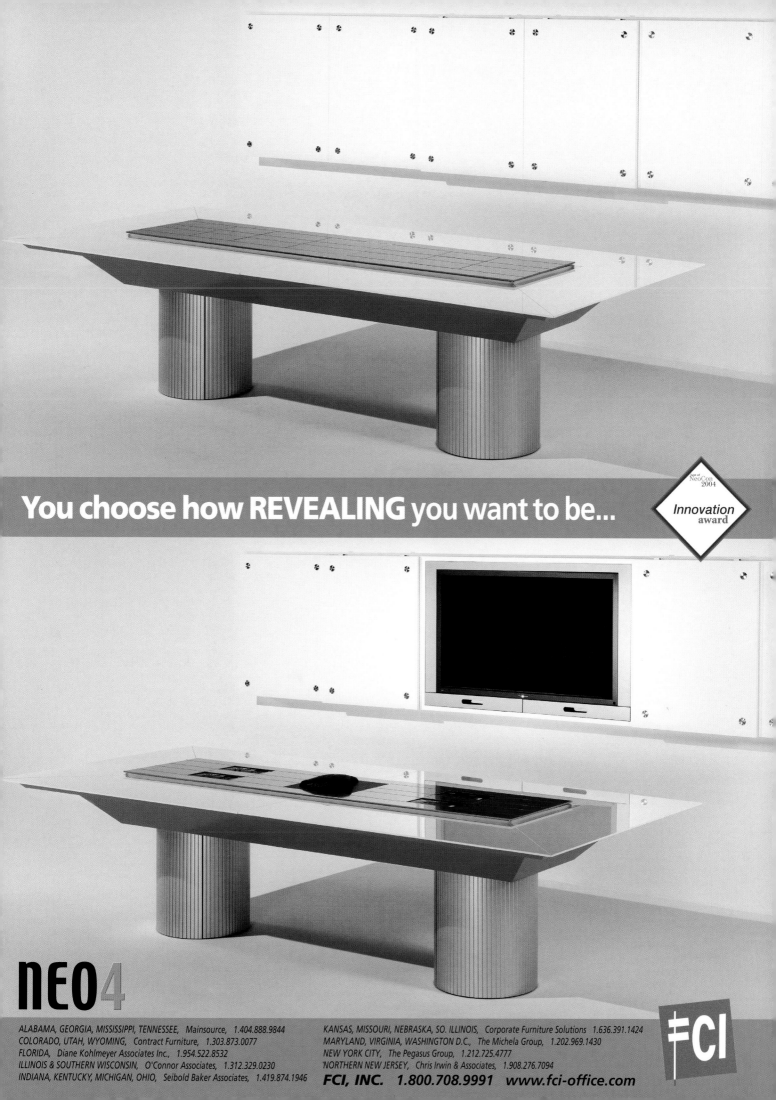

**Wallcoverings:** Delux Paints
**General Contractors:** Brennan Group

SAC Capital
**Design Firm:** Roger Ferris & Partners
**Furniture:** Bernhardt, Keilhauer, Knoll, Morrison & Repp, Steelcase, Tuohy
**Carpets & Flooring:** American Olean, Forbo, Interface
**Fabrics:** Maharam
**Lighting:** Belfer, Kurt Versen, Lucifer, Rambusch, Wila, Zumtobel Staff
**Ceilings:** Ceilings Plus, Decoustics, USG
**Wallcoverings:** Benjamin Moore
**General Contractors:** Bovis Lend Lease

Satellite Asset Management
**Design Firm:** Ted Moudis Associates
**Furniture:** HBF, Herman Miller
**Carpets & Flooring:** Marmoleum, Monterey, Stone Source, Tuva
**Fabrics:** Brentano, Designtex, Larsen
**Lighting:** Focal Point, Wila
**Ceilings:** Armstrong
**Wallcoverings:** Amian Custom, Benjamin Moore, Maharam, Scuffmaster
**General Contractors:** Corporate Interiors Contracting

Sempra - 83 Harvard - Metals
**Design Firm:** Roger Ferris & Partners
**Furniture:** Evans, Steelcase
**Carpets & Flooring:** Forbo, Interface
**Lighting:** Alcko, Elliptipar, Focal Point, Zumtobel Staff
**Ceilings:** Ceilings Plus
**Wallcoverings:** Benjamin Moore
**General Contractors:** A.P. Construction Corp.

Sonnenschein, Nath & Rosenthal
**Design Firm:** Perkins + Will
**Furniture:** Chemetal, Steelcase
**Carpets & Flooring:** Interface, Karastan, Quarry Tile, Sadler Tile
**Fabrics:** Formica, Knoll, Lamin-Art, Maharam, Nevamar
**Lighting:** Focal Point, Juno, Lightolier, Louis Poulsen, National Cathode
**Wallcoverings:** Benjamin Moore, Carnegie
**General Contractors:** Turner Construction Company

SS+K
**Design Firm:** JPC Architects
**Furniture:** Fleishmann
**Carpets & Flooring:** Shaw
**Lighting:** Energie
**General Contractors:** Pennon Construction Co.

Tandus Showroom
**Design Firm:** OWP/P
**Furniture:** Datesweiser, Herman Miller, Knoll
**Carpets & Flooring:** Tandus
**Fabrics:** Knoll
**Wallcoverings:** Benjamin Moore, Knoll
**General Contractors:** Alps Construction, Inc.

Target Corporation Headquarters
**Design Firm:** Ellerbe Becket, Inc.
**Furniture:** Artifex Millwork, Artifort, Bernhardt, Brayton, Fixtures Furniture, HBF, Keilhauer, Leland, Ligne Rossot, Morson Collection, Nienkamper, Offecet, Steelcase, Vecta
**Carpets & Flooring:** Atlas, Bolyu, Collins & Aikman, Constantine, Interface, Katelo Tile, Twin City Tile & Marble
**Fabrics:** Architex, Bernhardt, Brayton, Brentano, Carnegie, Designtex, Folio, Garret Leather, HBF, Knoll, Ligne Rosset, Maharam, Momentum, Paul Brayton, Unika Vaev, Vecta
**Lighting:** Akis, AV Mazzega, Illuminating Experiences, Winona
**Wallcoverings:** Carnegie, Guilford, Harmon, Herman Miller, Innovative, Knoll, MDC, Vycon
**General Contractors:** Ryan Companies US, Inc.

Telenor
**Design Firm:** NBBJ-HUS-PKA
**Furniture:** CGM, Fora Form, HAG ASA, Johansen Design, System B8 Mobler

**Wallcoverings:** Arbeidsfelleskapet BFP

Time Warner Center
**Design Firm:** Mancini-Duffy
**Furniture:** Davis, Dessin Fournir, Geiger, HBF, Herman Miller, ICF, Irwin Seating, Keilhauer, SR Wood, Troscan Design
**Carpets & Flooring:** Azrock, Bentley, Collins & Aikman, Edward Fields, Interface, Lees, Lonseal, Monterey, Prince Street, Stone Source, TexStyle
**Lighting:** Baldinger, Kurt Versen, Litecontrol, Zumtobel Staff
**Wallcoverings:** Benjamin Moore, Carnegie, DBF Scuffcoat, DeVoc, Designtex, Innovations, Jim Thompson, JM Lynne, Maharam, New Mat, Sherwin Williams
**General Contractors:** Turner Construction

Tosco
**Design Firm:** Perkins Eastman Architects
**Furniture:** Herman Miller
**Carpets & Flooring:** Bentley, Shaw, Woolshire
**Fabrics:** Carnegie, Herman Miller, Salamandre, Spinneybeck
**Ceilings:** Armstrong
**Wallcoverings:** Benjamin Moore, Cymbline, Designtex, Scuffmaster, Wolf Gordon
**General Contractors:** AP Construction

Umenohana Restaurant - Beverly Hills, Cal.
**Design Firm:** H. Hendy Associates
**Furniture:** CCS, David Furniture, WB Powell
**Carpets & Flooring:** Emser, Shaw, Terrazzo, Walker Zanger, Welson & York
**Fabrics:** Brayton, Carnegie, Edelman Leather, Guilford, Maharam, Pollack
**Lighting:** D-Form, Fox & Fox Design, Prudential
**Ceilings:** Preferred Ceilings
**Wallcoverings:** Duggan & Assoc., Frazee, ICI, MDC, Muraspec, Wolf Gordon
**General Contractors:** Jaisei Construction

Unilever ELT
**Design Firm:** Griswold, Heckel & Kelly Associates, Inc. (GHK)
**Furniture:** Brayton, Bernhardt, Danker, Gordon International, HBC, Keilhauer, OFS, Sellew & Douglas, Steelcase
**Carpets & Flooring:** Amtico, Atlas, Azrock, Bentley, Karastan
**Fabrics:** Carnegie, Joseph Noble, Luna, Yves Gonnet
**Lighting:** Lithonia, Tango Lighting
**Ceilings:** Armstrong
**Wallcoverings:** Carnegie, Innovations, Maharam, Zolatone
**General Contractors:** John Gallin & Son

Vanco Energy Company
**Design Firm:** DMJM Rottet
**Furniture:** David Edwards, Halcon, Herman Miller, Keilhauer, Knoll, Minotti
**Carpets & Flooring:** Constantine, National Terrazzo Tile & Marble, Luxica Enamel Flooring
**Fabrics:** Bernhardt, Edelman Leather, Knoll, Spinneybeck
**Lighting:** Belfer, H.E. Williams, Kurt Versen, Modular
**Ceilings:** Armstrong
**Wallcoverings:** Maharam, Pratt & Lambert
**General Contractors:** Constructors

A Venture Capital Firm
**Design Firm:** Gary Lee Partners
**Furniture:** Baker, Brayton, Caledonian, Conant, ICF, Knoll, Melrose House, Mike Bell, William Switzer
**Carpets & Flooring:** Bloomsburg, Botticcino Marble, Karastan
**Fabrics:** Bellinger, Edelman Leather, Great Plains, Joseph Noble, J. Robert Scott, Ralph Lauren, Scalamandre
**Lighting:** Columbia, Eureka, Halo, Kurt Versen, Light Control, Lucifer, Zumtobel Staff
**Ceilings:** USG
**Wallcoverings:** Benjamin Moore
**General Contractors:** Clune Construction Inc.

Vocational Guidance Services
**Design Firm:** Oliver Design Group
**Furniture:** Bretford, Falcon, Humanscale, Inscape, Keilhauer, Martin Brattrud, Prismatique, Source Intl, Steelcase, Vecta, Versteel
**Carpets & Flooring:** Armstrong, Dal-Tile, Durkan, Monterey, Tepromark

**Fabrics:** Anzea, Knoll, Unika Vaev
**Lighting:** Beyr, Hydrel, Indy Lighting, Lithonia, P.A.L., Peerless
**Ceilings:** Armstrong, USG
**Wallcoverings:** Benjamin Moore, Dal-Tile, ICI, Petrarch, Scuffmaster
**General Contractors:** Dunlop & Johnston, Inc.

Wachovia Calibre
**Design Firm:** Nelson
**Furniture:** Steelcase, Stowe-Davis
**Carpets & Flooring:** Durkan, Mohawk
**Fabrics:** Designtex, Maharam
**Lighting:** Artemide, National, Tango
**Ceilings:** Armstrong
**Wallcoverings:** Benjamin Moore, Maya Romanoff, Wolf Gordon
**General Contractors:** Magnolia Construction

Watson Wyatt Worldwide
**Design Firm:** Griswold, Heckel & Kelly Associates, Inc. (GHK)
**Furniture:** Bernhardt, Cartwright, Hayworth, Price Modern of Washington
**Carpets & Flooring:** Bentley, Johnsonite
**Fabrics:** Haworth, Knoll, Unika Vaev
**Lighting:** Dual Lite, IDC, Kurt Versen, Legion Lighting, Linear Lighting, Tsao Design, USA Illuminations, Zumtobel Staff
**Ceilings:** USG
**Wallcoverings:** Benjamin Moore
**General Contractors:** Lehr Construction Corp.

Watt Plaza Renovation
**Design Firm:** Wolcott Architecture Interiors
**Carpets & Flooring:** Serena Marble & Granite
**General Contractors:** Gregg Holwick Construction, Inc.

Weil Gotshal Manges
**Design Firm:** Gensler
**Furniture:** Aeron, Barbara Barry, Carmel, Creative Wood, HBF, Herman Miller, Knoll, Pucci, Spencer Fung Zen, Vida
**Carpets & Flooring:** Constantine
**Lighting:** Galussa, Gecko Designs

Winstead Sechrest & Minick
**Design Firm:** Susman Tisdale & Gayle
**Furniture:** David Edward, Halcon, HBF, Keilhauer
**Carpets & Flooring:** Crossely, Monterey, Solnhoffen
**Fabrics:** Garrett Leather, Ultra Suede
**Lighting:** Linear Lighting, Zumtobel Staff
**Ceilings:** USG
**Wallcoverings:** Benjamin Moore, TriKes
**General Contractors:** White Construction Company

Winthrop & Weinstine
**Design Firm:** Perkins + Will
**Furniture:** Bernhardt, David Edward, Kron, SMED
**Carpets & Flooring:** Constantine, Dal-Tile, Tilex Design
**Lighting:** Cooper-Halo Lighting, Indy Lighting, LBL Lighting, Wever & Ducre
**Wallcoverings:** Arborite, ICI
**General Contractors:** RJM Construction

Wolf, Greenfield & Sacks, P.C.
**Design Firm:** CBT/Childs Bertman Tseckares, Inc.
**Furniture:** Bernhardt, Epic, HBF, Keilhauer, Nienkamper, Vecta
**Carpets & Flooring:** Atlas, Constantine, Karastan, Kentucky Wood Flooring, Tuva
**Fabrics:** Designtex, HBF, Knoll, Luna, Maharam, Osborne + Little, Pollack, Spinneybeck, Testile Mania
**Lighting:** Louis Poulsen
**Ceilings:** Armstrong
**Wallcoverings:** Benjamin Moore, ICI, Sherwin Williams
**General Contractors:** Payton Construction

Zurich Capital Markets
**Design Firm:** Ted Moudis Associates
**Carpets & Flooring:** Hartco, Interface
**Fabrics:** Genji
**Lighting:** Leucos
**Ceilings:** Armstrong
**Wallcoverings:** Benjamin Moore, Tandem, Vescom
**General Contractors:** Structure Tone, Inc.

**THOUSANDS OF INTERIOR PRODUCTS & RESOURCES, THREE DAYS, ONE LOCATION — THE MERCHANDISE MART, CHICAGO**

# June 13-15, 2005

ALSO FEATURING:
BUILDINGS SHOW® • GREEN*LIFE*™
OFFICE EXPO BY OFDA • TECHNOCON™
NEWHOSPITALITY • FINE DESIGN RESIDENTIAL FURNISHINGS SHOW™

WWW.MERCHANDISEMART.COM • (800) 677-6278

# NeoCon®
## World's Trade Fair
SOLUTIONS FOR THE DESIGN AND
MANAGEMENT OF THE BUILT ENVIRONMENT

Less
designed by
Jean Nouvel

Naos System
designed by
Studio Cerri &
Associati

Progetto 25
designed by
Luca Meda

Unifor
149 Fifth Avenue
New York, NY 10010

Tel: 212.673.3434
Fax: 212.673.7317
unifor@uniforusa.com

# The Designer Series

HOSPITALITY & RESTAURANT DESIGN No. 3
ROGER YEE

Healthcare Spaces No.
Roger Yee

Corporate Interiors No. 6
Roger Yee

Educational Environments No. 2
Roger Yee

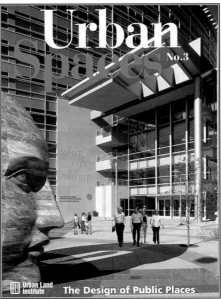

Urban Spaces No.3
Urban Land Institute
The Design of Public Places

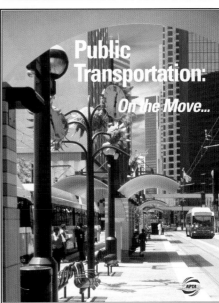

Public Transportation: On the Move...

# Visual Reference Publications, Inc.

302 Fifth Avenue, New York, NY 10001
Tel: 212.279.7000 • Fax: 212.279.7014
www.visualreference.com

BOYD

# Index by Projects